A TREATISE

ON

EPIZOOTIC LYMPHANGITIS

BY

CAPTAIN W. A. PALLIN, F.R.C.V.S.
ARMY VETERINARY DEPARTMENT

WITH ILLUSTRATIONS

NEW YORK
WILLIAM R. JENKINS
VETERINARY PUBLISHER AND BOOKSELLER
851 AND 853 SIXTH AVENUE
—
1905

CONTENTS

ILLUSTRATIONS

PREFACE

IN the following treatise I have endeavoured to combine my experiences with that of other writers on a subject which must be of great interest to the veterinary profession generally, especially in this country at the present moment, and it attempts to give a clear and complete account of a subject about which there is at present a paucity of English veterinary literature.

References to the literature on the subject have been freely made, but I wish to express my indebtedness to the works of NOCARD and LECLAINCHE, and TOKISHIGE, and also to state that I am greatly indebted to Professor BOYCE in permitting me to publish my work under the auspices of the University Press of Liverpool.

W. A. PALLIN

June, 1904

PREFACE TO THE SECOND EDITION

OWING to the favourable manner in which this little work has been received by the public, and more especially by the military authorities, a second edition has already been demanded to complete orders ; consequently, there has been little time for the purpose of revision, and with the exception of a few minor alterations and the addition of an index, the book is practically a reprint of the first edition.

W. A. PALLIN

September, 1904

EPIZOOTIC LYMPHANGITIS

INTRODUCTION

IN offering the following small work on this interesting subject to the public, I wish to explain that although I have not yet published anything about epizootic lymphangitis, I have nevertheless been collecting data and had some considerable experience of the disease in various parts of the world since the year 1899, when I first came in contact with it at a remount depôt in Northern India, where I had to deal with a very large outbreak for some fourteen months. Since then I have observed the disease in China in 1900-1901, Japan in 1901 in the form of preserved pathological and bacteriological specimens. In India again in 1902, and in Ireland in 1903 and 1904.

LITERATURE ON THE DISEASE

Until quite recently very little had been written about the disease, at least so far as English literature is concerned, and even now, a good clear concise account of the disease is not yet to be found in any of our standard books, although the disease has been recognized in England amongst army horses returning from South Africa since 1902, and since last autumn in Ireland also amongst army horses, and recently in London and other centres in England amongst private animals. The earliest reports I can find on the subject in English were made by Moore (in the *Veterinary Record* for 1896) who apparently had some cases of the diseases amongst government horses in Bengal in 1894. Evans appears to have studied the disease in Burma about the same

B

time, and their experiences are embodied in a pamphlet edited by Pease in 1897, who gives a detailed account of Moore's cases, but confounds them with another disease, viz., ' Ulcerative Lymphangitis.'   In later years the disease has been studied by Lingard in India (see *Annual Report*, 1900-1901), and quite recently articles have appeared in the *Veterinary Journals* by Holmes, Martin, Brodie-Mills, Hunting, MacFadyean, Head, Butler, Cranford, and others, and a small note on the disease also appears in Hayes's *Translation of Fried-berger and Fröhner*, Vol. I, at the end of the chapter on glanders, and Hayes also gives a short account of the disease in his last edition of *Veterinary Notes for Horse Owners*.   Since the foregoing remarks were penned, I find that Law in his new work, recently published, Bow-hill in his book on *Bacteriological Technique*, and Williams in his last edition of *Veterinary Surgery*, also describe the disease, but the clearest accounts of it have been written by the French veterinarians, Ed. Nocard and E. Leclainche, in their *Les Maladies Microbiennes des Animaux*, Vol. II, and by Tokishige in a pamphlet on *Japanese Farcy*, dated May, 1897, and it is from these two last works that most of the information as regards the history and early experiments on the disease have been obtained.   The latest addition to the literature on this subject in English is a paper written by Martin, which was discussed by the members of the National Veterinary Association at their Meeting, held in Dublin on the 16th and 17th August, 1904.

NATURE OF THE DISEASE

Epizootic lymphangitis is a virulent inoculable disease, characterized by suppuration of the superficial and subcutaneous lymphatic vessels, due to the presence of a specific organism. The disease is observed almost exclusively in solipeds, but Tokishige reports having seen it affecting cattle in Japan.

History

The disease has from time immemorial been invariably confounded with glanders (farcy) and ulcerative lymphangitis, in whatever part of the world it has appeared, and even with the assistance of mallein and modern science, veterinarians of nearly every nationality still continue to make the same mistakes. Since the commencement of the nineteenth century, about 1820, French veterinarians have recognized the disease under the names river farcy, *farcin en cul de poule*, curable or benign farcy, a particular form of farcy characterized by the appearance of sores exclusively on the skin, and any attempt that was made to classify the disease almost always resolved itself into simply recognizing it as glanders (farcy) of the skin. H. Bouley in an article dated 1860, recognizes no other diseases resembling glanders (farcy) except traumatic thrombosis of the lymphatics and the well-known complications of strangles and horse pox.

In 1865 Pearson studied the disease in Sweden, and he declared that the farcy of the north was not real farcy, but only a form of lymphangitis which yielded to treatment. Delormi, in 1867, described several cases of a benign form of farcy, which in no case terminated in glanders, and he hesitatingly questions the identity of true glanders and glanders (farcy) without ever suspecting the existence of any other form of farcy.

The question of the diagnosis was raised again in 1870 by French veterinary officers who observed a special form of epizootic farcy both in Algeria and France. Barrier Senior was of the opinion 'That the Algerian farcy was a particular disease of the lymphatic system,' and his statement to that effect was almost immediately challenged by Tixier and Delamotte, who were misled by the co-existence of glanders amongst their patients, and they finally concluded that African farcy was identical with glanders (farcy) and, in this respect, history has repeated itself over and over again, as both in India in 1899, and in South Africa during the recent war, the disease was confounded with glanders, and in many cases for that very same reason, viz., the co-existence of both diseases, the one recognized and the other (being unfamiliar) not recognized, until recently, as a separate disease. In France the unity of the different forms of farcy was acknowledged, and the African farcy was considered to be an attenuated form of glanders (farcy) until 1873, when Rivolta discovered the organism, viz., a cryptococcus.

In 1881 Chénier wrote an article explaining definitely the difference between farcy (glanders) and farcy (lymphangitis), pointing out that the latter disease only affects the lymphatic system and is not of the same nature as glanders, and that experimental inoculations of material from animals affected with the disease never produce true glanders. Finally, in 1883, Rivolta and Micellone published a paper containing a precise account of the nature of the disease ; they pointed out the constant presence in the pus from the nodules and cords of a particular organism, already described by Rivolta in 1873, in certain forms of farcy, and they state that there exists amongst horses a variety of farcy which may be called cryptococcic,

(1) Because it is produced and develops from a cryptococcus.

(2) Because the cryptococcus is always to be found in the abscesses and cords of the farcy.

(3) Because the cryptococcus is also to be found constantly in isolated pustules or originally deep seated in the skin and which have not yet come in contact with the air.

(4) Because inoculated into a healthy horse it multiplies prodigiously at the seat of inoculation where by degrees it gives rise to first a nodule, then a tumour, and then a tumefaction.

They then go on to state that the disease produced by this cryptococcus is the same as that described by the Frenchman, Chénier, several years before, under the name of African or river farcy.

Almost about the same time Bassi confirmed these new discoveries and reported some interesting clinical observations, and gave an account of some attempts at experimental inoculations. Since then 'epizootic lymphangitis' has formed the subject of several essays by French veterinary officers (namely, Jaubert, Quiclet, Debrade, Wiart, Peupion, Boinet, and Chauvrat). Peuch gives a similar description of the disease, and in 1891 Nocard also found the cryptococcus in the pus and tissues, and pointed out the diagnostic importance of the constant presence of the parasite, and how easily it can be found ; he also called attention to the existence in some cases of lesions on the mucous membranes resembling glanders.

Tokishige sat with a special Board of Commissioners in 1888, when they conducted experiments on this disease in Japan, where it has been known for years under the name of Japanese farcy. They reported having first found a characteristic bacillus identical with Schütz-Loeffler's bacillus, but in 1893 Tokishige found a second pathological germ which he described as a kind of

' saccharomyces,' and mentioned, at the same time, that these organisms were found both in horses and cattle presenting symptoms of Japanese farcy. According to this writer the disease has been known in Japan under different synonyms, *i.e.*, Japanese farcy (Hiso), Pseudo-farcy (Kasei-hiso), Equine Pox (Hoso), Equine Syphilis (Kasa), Inundation Fever (Gogue Netsu), Yakume (duty), Dekime (eruption), Inochitori (fatal), and he described it as a special kind of skin disease prevailing amongst horses and cattle, and states that the Japanese farmers believe that horses, especially foals, must in the natural course of events contract the disease, but that having once safely got over it the animal becomes not only immuned against another attack, but is stronger and more robust in its constitution, and con-sequently, owing to this fallacy, are considered more valuable—a common saying amongst Japanese farmers, who have a pony that has recovered, is literally trans-lated ' my pony has done his duty.' Mention of this only shows how wide-spread the disease is in that country. Formerly it was only known in the north-eastern part of Japan, more especially in Sendai and the neighbourhood, later on the disease gradually spread over a wide area towards the south-east, and subsequently it was found in nearly all the provinces of Japan : their statistics show a total number of 16,497 cases from 1887-95, an average of over one thousand cases per annum. It is said to prevail in low marshy districts and after inundations, also more in the rainy seasons than the dry, and more in the cold seasons than the hot. The ancient history of disease in Japan is quite unknown, a description of some form of skin disease called *so* or *wo* which appears to be similar to it is found in some of their old veterinary literature, which is mostly translated from the Chinese, but even then they (the Japanese) seem to think that the disease therein referred to was glanders, which they state is very common amongst Chinese ponies. My own experience in China in 1900-1901 goes to substantiate this statement, as glanders was found to be very common amongst Chinese ponies and mules in North China : yet cases of epizootic lymphangitis were also recognized by me, although I doubt very much if the Chinese themselves recognize more than one disease : a veterinary practitioner, whom I met out there, also only recognized glanders. However, Tokishige says the disease in Japan can be traced back many hundred years, and although it was naturally first thought to have been imported from China and Korea, the Japanese hearing later of the prevalence of the disease in Southern Europe and Africa were then more inclined to think that it came not from China but from Africa or Europe, and Tokishige, in a footnote, mentions that Masamune imported Persian horses into the north-east of Japan (but no date is given).

In India, as already stated, cases were recognized in 1894 by Moore, under the name of ulcerative lymphangitis, which, in my opinion, his experiments go to prove were really epizootic lymphangitis. It appears to have been well known in Burma for many years, but Lingard was the first to recognize the organism in India, and was of the opinion that the outbreaks in the remount depôts at Karnal and Hapur, in 1899, originated from mules imported from Italy in the previous year. But the history of the outbreak in the Hapur depôt, at least, goes to prove that the disease originated amongst the Indian country-bred horses, as no cases were recognized amongst the mules until several months after the disease had broken out amongst the horses ; there was nothing to show that any of the mules ever had any symptoms of disease previous to

the cases amongst the horses, and Lingard's assumption
was made simply on the fact that the disease was at
that time known in Italy, but not apparently known
to him to have previously existed in India. My
subsequent experience of the disease leads me to think
that it has been in India for years, unrecognized, and
confounded with glanders. I had personal experience
myself in this very same outbreak of so-called unsatisfactory results with mallein, and I am well aware that
many other similar experiences were also reported from
various parts of India, and that in each case the disease
being dealt with was not glanders but epizootic lymphangitis or both diseases co-existing. In many cases the
appearances, both *ante-mortem* and *post-mortem*, were
misleading—the (mallein) temperature charts were
occasionally unreliable and appeared at times to be
subject to climatic and local influences.

The disease next appears to have been imported
into South Africa during the war, as although it had
been known in Algiers and Egypt for many years
before that, there is no record of it being in South
Africa previous to the war ; however, seeing how per-
sistently it has been confounded with glanders, it may
have been there all the time unrecognized ; in any case,
there was ample opportunity during the war for the
disease being imported into the country by remounts
from all over the world, *e.g.*, Southern Europe and
India, these being known centres of the disease at the
time.

From South Africa the disease, as before stated,
has been imported into England and Ireland by government horses returned from the Cape ; the first case
was, I understand, detected at Aldershot, in 1902, and
the first case detected in Ireland was, curiously enough,
recognized by me at the Curragh, in October, 1903, and

outbreaks have now occurred at several centres throughout England and Ireland.

The spread and continued existence of this disease amongst army horses in Great Britain and Ireland is causing considerable anxiety to civilian horse-owners, and has been the subject matter of several important questions being raised about it in the House of Commons during the last three months.

The army statistics on the subject, made up to the 28th July, 1904, shew that up to date there have been—

In England 21 centres of infection.
„ Ireland 9 „ „
––
Total 30 „ „

Cured.	Remaining.	Destroyed.	Total.
32	108	254	394

Geographical Distribution

In France the disease was formerly known in a number of regions, particularly in the south-east; it was first known by the name of river farcy on account of it being more particularly noticed amongst the horses employed in towing boats on the rivers and canals. It spread from the south to the north and invaded the eastern and central departments, and from 1850 it was confounded with glanders and was dealt with as such in so far as sanitary precautions were concerned, but new centres kept appearing in the French cavalry which became infected more or less directly from horses imported from Algeria, where the disease was known to exist; it still exists in Southern France, and until recently was also to be found in the Maritime Alps and in Le Var.

In Sweden it is known as 'Norlander Rotz,' and according to Delarne and Norrland it was formerly quite common in some provinces. Lindqvist states it still exists in Finland, and it is said that he recognized the cryptococcus of Rivolta in 1871.

In Russia, some sixteen cases were reported amongst horses in 1896, and twenty-six more in 1897, all from a village in the province of Novgorod ; it is also reported from the province of Olonetz, where it is more inclined to take the nasal form, and as a result caused frequent slaughter of horses considered to be glandered.

In Italy a curable or benign form of farcy has been known for quite a long time under the names of Naples or Neapolitan farcy and *Mal del Verme*, and was apparently so common that Professor Caparini is said to have stated at Naples that farcy is a disease so common that people who are absolutely ignorant about medicine might almost recognize it at first sight, and 1,200 horses are stated to have been treated for the disease at the Naples Clinique during the space of five years. Bassi also reports a number of cases at Turin. In Algiers the disease is well-known in several regions both amongst horses and mules.

In Egypt, Bosso reported a number of cases at Cairo in 1875, and I understand that the disease is still met with there and known under the name of Saurago, and by the Arabs as 'El djedre,' as distinguished from glanders farcy, ' Bou-cha K'ar ' or ' Bow-achem.' The disease is also known in the Dutch Indies (Java and Bali) under the name of ' Patèk.'

Nocard and Leclainche state that the disease is also known in Gaudaloupe, where they say that it and glanders decimate the mule population.

Tokishige also mentions having seen the disease amongst cattle in Japan ; that it is not altogether rare, and that, although there are some differences in the symptoms observed in cattle and in the horse, the saccharomyces appear to be the same.

Zschokke and Nocard also make mention of a disease affecting cattle in Gaudaloupe, viz., bovine farcy or facin du boeuf ; but Nocard appears to have found that this disease (in cattle) was due to a streptothrix with which he inoculated guinea-pigs, oxen, and sheep, but horses, asses, dogs, and rabbits were found to be immune. Thus this would appear to be quite a different disease from epizootic lymphangitis in solipeds, and also from that noticed by Tokishige amongst cattle in Japan.

According to Nocard and Leclainche there have been no cases of the disease noticed in Central Europe ; and Tokishige pointed out that there was no mention of it either in English, German, or American literature.

BACTERIOLOGY

The cryptococcus is found abundantly in the morbid tissues and products, partly free in the plasma and partly enclosed in pus corpuscles, which are often loaded with ten or even twenty to thirty of them, causing the corpuscles to be sometimes double or triple their normal size. It is a slightly ovoid body, one end of which is generally pointed and the other rounded. It is characterized by its clearly defined contour and its very refractile double outline.

It measures about 3 to 4 μ in diameter, and in unstained preparations is best seen with a one-twelfth oil immersion and an Abbé condenser under a magnification of not less than eight hundred to one thousand diameters, particular attention being paid to the regulating of the light ; in stained specimens the organism can be easily seen under a much lower power.

The classification of the parasite has been discussed by several writers on the subject. Canalis puts it in the group of coccidia, Piana and Galli-Vallerio amongst the sporozoa, and Formi and Aruch in the blastomycetes, but Tokishige was the first to express the opinion that it was a class of saccharomyces, and Marcone, being of the same opinion, was anxious to change the name of the disease then already well-known as epizootic lymphangitis to *Saccharomycosis farciminosus*(Rivolta), and as these two observers both claimed to have cultivated the organism I am inclined to accept their opinion and adopt their nomenclature.

According to Tokishige the organism is provided with a thick membrane, the contents of which are more or less homogeneous and transparent or finely granular, and usually a coccus-like granule measuring ·25 to 1 μ in diameter is suspended in it.

The granule is either colourless or faintly yellow, has a strong refractive power, and performs a lively molecular movement, wandering in the contents, and generally found near one pole. Sometimes also collapsed semi-lunar cells are found ; these, he says, are probably old varieties whose contents have been evacuated.

Although somewhat smaller than the yeast of beer, Tokishige drew attention to the fact that it was a vegetable organism resembling the yeast fungus, and belonged to the order of saccharomyces. Fermi and Aruch both disagree with him on this, and point out that it does not ferment sugar.

STAINING

This is said by almost every writer on the subject to be difficult, and even by Nocard himself, who appears to have been the first to stain the organism. He recommends both the Gram-Nicolle and Gram-Weigert-Kuhne methods, but since the disease was first recognized in Ireland, during last October, I have to state from information gained from an unpublished note that Mettam was the first to show how easily really the organism could be stained by either of these methods, also that by a modification of the latter, he claims to have had the most satisfactory results.—*Vide Veterinary Record*, June 25, 1904. And I may here state that in doubtful cases staining is invaluable for absolute accuracy and expedience in diagnosing the presence or otherwise of the organism in a specimen from a suspected wound or abscess.

Nocard and Leclainche state that carbol-fuchsin stains the organism after long contact, and they also mention that Loeffler's method for staining cilia may also be resorted to.

Recently the organism has been also stained by the Claudius method, and in this connexion the name of Bowhill should be mentioned as having been the first to recommend it.—*Vide Veterinary Record*, January 9, 1904. For the convenience of my readers the following information regarding the technique of the best methods of staining the organism are given, together with the composition of the reagents required :—

(1) Nicolle's Violet—

    Saturated solution of gentian violet in 90 per cent.
      alcohol . . . . 10 c.c.
    1 per cent. aqueous solution carbolic acid . . 100 c.c.

(2) Nicolle's Thionine—

    Saturated solution of thionine in 90 per cent. alcohol 10 c.c.
    1 per cent. aqueous solution of carbolic acid . 100 c.c.

(3) Solution for Gram-Weigert-Kuhne's method—

    Concentrated solution of crystal violet . . . 1 part.
    Distilled water, to which a few drops of hydrochloric
      acid have been added . . . . . 10 parts.

(4) Gram's Iodine solution (Lugol's solution)—

Iodine	1 part.
Iodide of potassium	2 parts.
Distilled water	300 parts.

(5) Kuhne's Iodine solution—

Iodine	2 parts.
Iodide of potassium	4 parts.
Distilled water	100 parts.

(6) Zeihl's solution, 'carbol-fuchsin'—

Fuchsin	1 gramme
Absolute alcohol	10 c.c.
5 per cent. aqueous solution of carbolic acid	100 c.c.

(7) Counter stain—

Saturated solution of vesuvine (Bismarck brown).

(8) Decolourizing agents—

Alcohol or aniline oil.

(9) Clarifying agents—

Zylol or clove oil.

(10) Mounting agents—

Canada balsam or Farrant's solution.

Gram-Nicolle method.

Make a thin smear of pus from the suspected wound, ulcer or pustule, on a cover-glass or slide, fix it in the ordinary manner by passing it three times through the flame, and then proceed to stain either with No. 1 or No 2 solution, leaving it on for about five minutes ; then run it off, removing the superfluous stain by waving it for a moment or two in water, and put on the No. 4 solution, which fixes the stain in the organism. After leaving this on for about two or three minutes, run it off and treat with alcohol, which takes the stain out of everything except the various organisms which have

taken it up ; in fact it will begin to remove it from
the cryptococci also if left on more than a few seconds.
Having now decolourized put on the No. 7 solution (the
counter stain), and after having left this on for about
three minutes run it off, wash in water, and dry. The
specimen is now ready to be examined under the
microscope and may be mounted in Canada balsam.

Gram-Weigert-Kuhne method.

1. Stain with the No. 3 solution for five to fifteen
minutes.
2. Wash in water.
3. Dry with blotting paper.
4. Treat with the No. 5 iodine solution for one
to two minutes.
5. Dry with blotting paper.
6. Carefully decolourize with aniline oil.
7. Treat with zylol, and mount in Canada balsam.
Sections may be stained by this method, but they first
require staining for half-an-hour with lithium carmine
solution (carmine 2·5 to 100 parts of saturated solution
of lithium carbonate). Differentiate in alcohol or hydro-
chloric acid alcohol, then wash in water and proceed as
before.

Mettam's modification of the above method
principally consists in using hot carbol-fuchsin instead of
the No. 3 solution. He points out the advantage of
occasionally examining the specimens under the microscope to see how decolourization is progressing, and
the necessity of checking the action of the aniline oil
by thoroughly washing with zylol before the organisms
are completely decolourized, or only appear as red
rings, as they are very apt to do. He also recommends
fixing the specimen in alcohol in preference to heat.

Claudius method.

Stain with a 1 per cent. aqueous solution of methyl violet for two minutes, wash and place in a half-saturated solution of picric acid for one or two minutes. Decolourize with chloroform or clove oil, then treat with zylol and mount in Canada balsam.

NOTE.—In staining this organism the iodine solution may, with advantage, be made stronger ; in fact, to be accurate for the Gram-Nicolle method, the solution should be :—iodine, 1 part ; iodide of patassium, 2 parts ; and distilled water, 200 parts.

Also note that when the specimens are treated with alcohol they are very much inclined to fade, so that if one wishes to preserve them the methods in which alcohol is used are not to be recommended, and consequently it will be easily understood that better results are obtainable with a strong mordant and the use of aniline oil as a decolourizing agent ; in any case it will be noticed that there are almost invariably a certain number of organisms in the field which have not taken up the stain at all, and others which are only partially stained. The fact that the organism in a stained specimen can be seen in all three conditions in the one field has been claimed to be an advantage rather than a disadvantage, as some writers on the subject might lead one to suppose. Tokishige states that the young saccharomyces, which are full of protoplasm, easily take aniline stains, while those which contain fluid plasma never take the usual bacterial stains, and also that those granules which are free in the liquor puris can never be stained.

While on the subject of staining, I might mention that all the stains required can now be obtained ready-made in the form of tabloids, together with detailed instructions for use of the same. These preparations are most convenient and very portable.

According to Tokishige the organism is reproduced by budding. The cells become elongated, and after about a week they become dilated, the central granule enlarges and divides into two or more daughter granules of a faintly yellowish colour and homogenous quality. The swollen microbe often attains a diameter of 6 to 7 and even 12·45 μ and the granule 2·5 μ. After a time the swollen microbe assumes an oblong, cylindrical or dumb-bell form, and then by partition it is divided into two, three, or more segments, and finally develops into a kind of hyphae; secondary hyphae appear in the course of time also by budding, and afterwards tertiary hyphae appear from these.

Plate I shows the organism as demonstrated by Tokishige from the so-called Japanese farcy.

Plate II shows the organism from a preparation prepared and stained by Professor Mettam, of the Royal Veterinary College of Ireland.

Plate III shows a pustule in varying stages, and also the lesions in the subcutaneous tissues, from a photo by Tokishige.

CULTURE

This is obtained with difficulty. The growth is always slow, and develops much better in an acid than alkaline medium, the temperature not appearing to have any marked effect. Tokishige obtained a growth in peptonized bouillon, agar-agar, nutrient gelatine, and on potato.

In bouillon, after seventeen days, a white flaky deposit, which includes hyphae and cells, makes its appearance. On agar, after thirty days, the vegetation first becomes apparent in the form of greyish-white grains, and in from forty to fifty days a single colony

c

attains a diameter of 1 to 4 mm., and becomes distinctly prominent over the surface of the medium. In a full grown colony the surface is wrinkled, the colony is very dense and difficult to dissect with a platinum wire or crush under a cover-glass.

Microscopically, it consists of conglomerated masses, composed of hyphae, spherical bodies, and a number of free granules. The addition of grape sugar or glycerine to the medium has no influence on the vegetation.

On nutrient gelatine the vegetation takes place more on the upper strata, and in fifty-six days some yellowish-white sandy masses of an irregular shape, measuring 1 to 4 mm. in diameter, make their appearance. The gelatine does not liquefy except by heating, when the colony sinks and its growth stops.

On potato the growth is more rapid, and the colonies are of a light-brown colour, but otherwise they resemble the growths obtained on agar-agar.

Fluid media may also be used for the cultivation of this organism, but peptone must be added. Tokishige states that it neither grows on an infusion of horse dung or hay, nor in a solution of sugar.

Marcone cultivated the cryptococcus on horse serum mixed with 2 per cent. solution of agar-agar, glycerine and cane sugar, and got after fifteen days, at a temperature of from 32°-37° centigrade, some fine greyish specks making their appearance and slowly enlarging at several points of the medium ; the growth then appears to cease and falls to the bottom of the flask, where it forms a thick, uniform, white deposit.

When the culture is old, if the flask be shaken, it becomes opaque, and does not clear up for some considerable time.

As might be anticipated, the cryptococci or saccharomyces are often associated with staphylococci, diplococci or streptococci, and other organisms, which are especially met with in the contents of the pustules and abscesses and in the lymphatic glands.

Plate IV shows a culture made by Tokishige.

INCUBATIVE PERIOD

My experience is that this may be put down as anything varying from three weeks to three months, and it may extend to six, eight, or ten months, and even more ; in fact, I have one case on record which had an incubative period of over thirteen months. I have also a few cases on record in which the disease recurred after being apparently cured, but in none of these did the second incubative period exceed one month ; still there appears to be no reason why the incubative period for recurrent cases should differ very much from that of ordinary ones, and Cranford, writing from India, records a case which recurred after fourteen months (*Veterinary Record*, June 4, 1904).

In my experimental cases the first symptoms of the disease (viz., a nodule) appeared after thirty-two days, with pustules bursting on the fifty-third day ; mode of inoculation being subcutaneous. Mettam, experimenting on the disease recently, informs me that he did not get the nodular symptoms until after forty days, that pustules formed and burst five days afterwards, and that the lesions had all healed again and disappeared in a couple of weeks' time after the pustules burst, but that now (1st April, 1904), three months afterwards, the nodules are reappearing. The mode of inoculation in this case was scarification made in two separate places, one on the near side of the neck which took, and another on the off quarter which up to date shows no sign of the disease.

Tixier, Delamotte, and Chauvrat by puncture and scarification got pustules in from twenty to sixty-six days. Delamotte and Peuch state the period in donkeys is a month or more. Wiart gives the period as eight days to five or six months. Quiclet has seen it take eighty-nine days to develop, and Tokishige makes no attempt to specify any time.

Symptoms

The symptoms are usually found on the skin, but occasionally occur on the mucous membrane, and may extend to the internal organs. I have personally observed the disease in the following regions, viz. :—

Head—Eyes (conjunctiva), muzzle, nose, face, cheeks, lips, submaxillary space, orbital process, and inside the external ear.

Neck—Various parts.

Trunk—Withers, shoulders, back, loins, chest, sides, flank, croup, quarters, hips, tail, anus, vulva, perineum, scrotum, and sheath.

Fore and Hind Limbs—Various parts, from coronet upwards.

Mucous Membrane—Lining of alae of nostrils, septum, nasi, sinuses of the head, pharynx, larynx, and trachea.

(1) *Cutaneous variety.*

In Plates V, VI, VII, VIII, IX, X, XI, and XII, taken from photographs of cases observed by the author, the lesions will be seen in a number of the sites mentioned.

As will be seen from the foregoing remarks, the lesions may be found on any part of the body, but they are most frequently associated with those parts which are most exposed to wounds from kicks, contusions, and harness galls.

Inoculation apparently almost invariably takes place from wounds, and may therefore develop from the slightest abrasion.

The disease usually first shows itself at the seat of a pre-existing wound, or it may develop from a wound not yet healed ; in the former case, the only thing that is generally noticed at first is that a small pustule has broken out on the edge of an old scar, or adjacent to it ; on closer examination tumefaction is generally found to exist around the place, and cording and knotting of the adjacent lymphatic vessels may also usually be felt so clearly that even from the beginning they may be frequently seen from a distance. But the time required for all these various symptoms to develop varies greatly ; sometimes when a limb is the seat of the disease, the whole leg may suddenly swell up like an ordinary case of lymphangitis, and no cording or nodules may be recognized until the acute inflammation and diffuse swelling have subsided. At other times, the corded lymphatics may be noticed some considerable time before any pustules make their appearance, and a long chain of nodules may be seen extending along the course of the lymphatics of a limb, or, if situated on the head, neck, or trunk, they radiate towards the nearest lymphatic glands.

The nodules vary in size, from a pea to a hen's egg ; they are well-defined, and at first hard and indurated, but as the disease runs its course, they soften ; the time required for this change is very irregular, and principally depends upon the resistance of the surrounding tissues.

Along the course of the lymphatic vessels affected, pustules and abscesses are formed, which burst and discharge a thick, yellow pus, stained with blood ; the abscesses now continue to discharge, and their cavities become filled up with exuberant granulations, which, protruding beyond the surface of the skin (the edges of which are inclined to become inverted), form bright red fungoid (rosette) growths, which bleed easily when touched, and very much resemble farcy buds. Wounds which become infected with the disease may either heal up and then break out again, or they may gradually take on the appearance of the sores just described.

The buds, ulcers, or sores, by all of which names they are known, are characterized by their bright red exuberant granulations and their fungoid appearance, as well as by their indurated base and well-defined edges ; the adjoining skin, which is partially inverted, has a peculiar shiny appearance ; an opening exists in the centre of the bud, from which the pus, at first creamy, and afterwards yellowish, oily, and curdled, is continually discharging.

Careful examination of these buds or sores will show that they are really quite different from those of glanders (farcy), and that with energetic treatment they have an inclination to heal.

The disease is commonest in the limbs, and will be found in the fore-leg generally extending up along the fore-arm to the anti-brachial region and point of shoulder as seen in Plates VI, VII, and VIII, or, if it extends from the elbow (frequently seen as a sequel to capped elbows), it extends across the caput muscles. In the hind limbs it has a great tendency to extend along the inside of the thigh, as seen in Plates IX and X (where wounds due particularly to kicks are frequently situated), to the groin, and from thence it may wind round the back of the thigh or extend along the belly. The writer has seen an animal with as many as thirty-three sores, varying from the size of a sixpence to a five-shilling piece and larger, on one limb. The majority of cases observed by me in the fore-limb were developed from broken knees and wounds (principally caused by kicks) on the inside of the fore-arm ; these cases in developing extend as a rule, rather deeply seated, up along the flexor brachii muscle to the point of shoulder, and often exhibit nodules as large as a hen's egg, as seen in Plate VIII.

Numerous cases of infection after castration and strangles were observed. Those following castration were most difficult cases to deal with as schirrus cord supervened, and the scrotum and sheath became greatly enlarged, indurated, and infiltrated with new formations and multiple abscesses.

Plate XI shows the disease on the edge of the vulva, and extending to the perinaeum, and mammary gland.

Those following strangles, as seen in Plate XII, were also greatly protracted, the submaxillary glands and submaxillary space became the seat of multiple abscesses, and the disease extended round the jaw to the cheek along the course of Steno's duct, which also frequently became involved.

After affecting a cure, numerous chains of cicatrices may remain, sheaths of tendons, and joints may also become affected, causing chronic thickenings and enlargements, and the value of the animals to be greatly depreciated. Tokishige mentions a large number of cases occurring in Japan affecting the testicles, which is probably accounted for by the fact that the Japanese seldom or never castrate their horses (ponies), and when large numbers of them are collected together (such as in the army) wounds from kicks and scratches on the scrotum are no doubt very common.

(2) *Mucous membrane variety.*

Lesions of the disease on the mucous membrane have been noticed by me in some 7 to 10 per cent. of cases, *e.g.*, on the membrane, covering the lining of alae of nostrils, covering septum nasi and nasal organs, lining the sinuses of the head, the pharynx, larynx, and upper third of trachea, and also on the conjunctiva. I am inclined to think that the percentage of cases observed by me in these parts is probably above the average, although Tokishige relates quite a number of cases in which the mucous membranes were the seat of the disease.

Plates XIII, XIV, XV, and XVI show very clearly the lesions as they were seen in some of those parts, and I may here mention that in each case the diagnosis was verified by microscopical examination, that of Plate XIII being also tested with mallein gave no reaction, nor were any lesions of glanders recognized in the lungs of any of them.

The lesions in the nose have been observed by me both uni-lateral and bi-lateral, and a tendency for them to become bi-lateral was noticed to prevail. Some writers on the subject state that, in contrast to glanders, the lesions are only found in the lower third of the nasal chambers. I have noticed myself that it is certainly commonest only in that portion, but have ample proof to show that most extensive lesions of the disease (unaccompanied by glanders) may occasionally be found in all the nasal chambers, and that they may also extend to the pharynx, larynx, and trachea.

Nocard and Leclainche state that the lesions in the nose are almost always bi-lateral, that they may extend to the pharynx, larynx, and trachea, and, in exceptional cases, to the large bronchial tubes. I might here mention that in addition to a few characteristic cutaneous cases

of the disease observed in North China in 1900 and
1901 amongst Chinese ponies and mules, I also saw in
addition to marked glanders cases, several other cases of
so-called glanders, showing most extensive lesions on the
nasal mucous membrane very much resembling glanders,
but there was no submaxillary glandular enlargement;
they did not re-act to mallein, and no glanders lesions
could be detected in the lungs or other internal organs
on post-mortem examination. Many of these cases
proved fatal in a very short time, and for want of a
better name I considered that they were a form of
pseudo-glanders; since then, however, I have seen a
case of epizootic lymphangitis exhibit very similar
symptoms; the disease running a very acute course, and
rapidly becoming generalized, the animal had to be destroyed. I often wonder if the cases seen in North China
could, possibly, have been of the same nature, or if they
were due to some other organism, *e.g.*, some form of
Pasteurella. Anyhow, whatever the disease was, it
caused many differences of opinion, especially amongst
the German veterinary officers. Mallein was, on many
occasions, again blamed for so-called unsatisfactory
results, and few seem to have recognized the possibility
of two diseases, *i.e.*, glanders and some other disease
closely resembling it clinically (with which we were
unfamiliar), being present and co-existing in many
cases.

The lesions on the nasal mucous membrane are
first noticed in the form of small papules or pimples,
which rapidly form into vesicles and burst, forming a
well-defined ulcer with a raised edge and dug-out
centre as seen in Plates XIII and XIV. They are at
first isolated, but later become confluent, and tend to
extend to the cartilage of the septum nasi, causing the
mucous membrane to become discoloured and greatly

thickened by exuberant granulations, at times forming a kind of polypus, which interferes with the respirations and causes snuffling. In advanced cases the cartilage becomes spongy and the nasal bones necrosed. Enlargement of the submaxillary glands may, but does not necessarily, as is stated in glanders, accompany nasal symptoms, *i.e.*, it is not constant, and frequently does not occur even in advanced cases ; however, when it is involved, the gland may be somewhat indurated and stiff from suppurative inflammation either affecting it or the surrounding tissues, but it is generally movable and seldom or never fixed to the jaw and knotty as in glanders.

In cases where the conjunctiva is the original seat of the disease, no symptoms may be noticed externally for several weeks after the disease has begun to develop ; but as it spreads towards the edge of the eyelid, a slight watery or purulent discharge may be the first thing detected, and on examination of the conjunctiva a pale pink, flat, fungoid granulation will be discovered under one of the lids or on the membrana nictitans—varying in size according to the age of the lesion. In one case (Plate XVII) which I observed, the granulation was about the size of the top of a pencil when first noticed, and there was no discharge or outward symptom of the disease for weeks, and it could only be seen when the eyelid was forcibly inverted. As the case developed the granulation spread ; as soon as it began to protrude beyond the edge of the eyelid the other symptoms then developed fairly rapidly; there was then profuse discharge from the eye, the whole conjunctiva became inflamed, and later the adjacent lymphatic vessels became affected ; the head on the same side became greatly swollen, the disease spread towards the orbital process, and the case was shortly afterwards destroyed. In other cases it continues indefinitely simply confined to the conjunctiva, or it may spread down the lachrymal duct to the nose.

When the nasal lesions are slight, there is an absence of discharge from the nose, but later on a thin fluid, mucous, muco-purulent, or sanious discharge develops, presently accompanied by an unpleasant odour from the breath.

General Symptoms

Except in those cases where the disease is ushered in by the ordinary symptoms of acute lymphangitis, there are very seldom any systemic changes accompanying the disease, at least in its early changes, nor for weeks or months after it has developed. The temperature generally remains normal, but in some cases there may be an inclination to very slight intermittent fever, which seldom runs above 102°, and only recurs about every ten days. The appetite is seldom or never impaired, and except in very advanced cases, which tend to become generalized, there is no loss of condition ; in fact, the disease seems to thrive best on animals in good condition in which the lymphatics are well developed and in good working order ; however, in deference to the foregoing symptoms, and those usually described, I have to state that I have seen the disease, in at least one verified case, rapidly develop and run a very acute course, in which the whole system was affected. The cases from which Plates No. XIV, XV, and XVI were obtained is the one in point. The subject was a five-year-old Arab trooper, admitted into hospital with simple fever, temperature 103·4. In the course of a few days symptoms of purpura haemorrhagica began to develop, the nose and extremities became oedematous,

and the temperature continued to vary from 103 to
104. The pulse was accelerated, the mucous membranes were injected and presented a few petechiae, and
the appetite was impaired. The case was treated for
purpura, but in the course of about three weeks ulcerations were detected on the pituitary membrane, and
simultaneous with these symptoms a profuse discharge
from both nostrils developed, marked enlargement of
the left submaxillary gland (on which side the ulcerations
on the mucous membrane were first noticed) was
also present, *but the gland was quite movable.* The
body became covered all over with a number of pimples
about the size of a pea, something similar to urticaria, there
being no particular arrangement ; the swellings of the
extremities, particularly the hind limbs, increased, but
cording of the lymphatics was altogether absent, and the
temperature continued to vary from 103 to 104. The
case was isolated with a view to being tested with mallein,
but after ten days, as the temperature remained up, and
as the case was rapidly becoming much worse (being
greatly emaciated, and now almost in a dying condition),
it was destroyed. At this time the ulcerations on the
mucous membranes were extending, respirations were
increased, the profuse dirty, sticky, blood-stained
discharge from the nostrils increased daily ; the pimples
all over the body had formed into vesicles, which had
rapidly broken out and discharged, more particularly
on the backs of the tendons of the hind legs, which
thereby assumed the appearance of an advanced case
of glanders. Microscopical examinations of the pus
from the tissues and from scrapings of the ulcerations
on the pituitary membrane revealed the cryptococci,
but no lesions of glanders could be detected either in
the lungs or in any other part of the body. This case
was more like glanders than any other verified case of

epizootic lymphangitis that I have seen, and, previous to destruction, I had certainly come to the conclusion that it was a case of glanders, although I already knew from practical experience that the ulcerations on the mucuous membranes had the typical appearance of the epizootic lymphangitis, and the submaxillary gland, although enlarged, was still easily movable.

I am indebted to Dr. Lingard for verifying the diagnosis of this case by microscopical examination of specimens taken from the nasal mucous membrane, submaxillary gland, and lungs. I might also mention that there was no glanders in the corps to which the horse belonged, and that this proved to be the forerunner of a series of other cases of epizootic lymphangitis in the unit, none of which terminated in glanders, so I feel convinced that there was no glanders complication. This case was noticed by me in India during the hot weather of 1902, and I have gone somewhat into detail to show how much some cases of this disease may simulate glanders, and how easily mistakes in diagnosis may occur if the microscopical examination is not carried out, *even by those who may think that they are thoroughly acquainted with the disease.* The cases referred to as seen in North China amongst ponies and mules, which I then called pseudo-glanders, were very similar to the case just described, and are now thought to be possibly the same, although they were even much more acute.

Tokishige states that the disease is always of long duration, and may last for months, and even years ; that acute cases in the true sense of the word never occur, and that the disease only assumes an acute character when it spreads over a large area of the skin, and also to the mucous membranes lining the respiratory track. In the slighter cases and even in many advanced ones the animal is generally able to do its ordinary work, but when the nasal symptoms develop or cutaneous symptoms are far advanced, the animal quickly falls off in condition, and emaciation sets in, followed by cachexia and death.

Symptoms in Cattle

According to Tokishige, also, the following are the symptoms found in Japan amongst cattle affected with a disease which he recognized as being caused by the saccharomyces, in 1890, viz. :—

The nodules are distributed all over the surface of the body without any particular arrangement, contrary to those seen amongst solipeds, in which the nodules are in beaded chains ; they form clearly-defined, indolent lumps, varying from the size of a hazel nut to that of a walnut. The development is much slower than in the horse, and the nodules take three times as long to come to a head and burst.

In referring to the disease in cattle, care should be taken not to confound it with a disease found amongst cattle in Gaudaloupe, known under the name of *farcin du boeuf*, and due to a bacillus discovered by Nocard, and which Metschnikoff describes as a streptothrix. This disease is only transmissible to cattle, sheep, and guinea-pigs, but does not affect horses or donkeys.

Post-Mortem Lesions

The corded and beaded lymphatics observed are simply inflamed lymphatic vessels, with their thickened walls, their internal membrane is congested, and the ducts are blocked with thick-clotted lymph mixed with pus, which is followed by the formation of the abscesses (pustules) and granulating sores. The affected parts are

found to be indurated and thickened by the formation of
fibrous tissue resulting from the chronic inflammation
set up by the disease. As already stated, the ulcerations on the mucous membrane are characterized by
their round, well-defined, raised borders and dug-out
appearance. They are at first isolated, but later become
confluent, and have as a rule a great tendency to granulate, and in advanced and severe cases the mucous
membrane is either greatly thickened or may be stripped
off the cartilage, which becomes gelatinous and spongy,
and both it and bone eventually become diseased.
I have seen the ulcerations extend to the pharynx,
larynx, and upper third of the trachea, and to the
sinuses of the head, and Nocard and Leclainche add
that they may extend to the large bronchi, and that
occasionally specific lesions are found in the lungs.
Tokishige mentions that lesions of the disease are found
in the lungs, but they are very rare, and he points out
that in many incidental cases lesions of chronic pneumonia,
pleuro-pneumonia, and pneumonia are occasionally
found on *post-mortem* examination co-existing. He
also mentions that in a few cases grey nodules resembling those of glanders are found, but he goes on to
state that when the saccharomyces are present the
lesions are in the form of a lobular pneumonia, con-
sisting of an interstitial cell infiltration around the bron-
chioli and alveoli. He also states having found the
disease in the liver and spleen. The lesions noticed by
me in the lungs have been confined to secondary
strangles, abscesses, patches of indurated pneumonia,
and numerous small hard nodules varying from the
size of a pin's head to a pea. These, in many cases,
very much resembled glanders, but they were not
surrounded by a hyperaemic zone ; they were invariably
calcareous and never caseous. Sections of these various

lesions under the microscope never revealed glanders, and mallein testing and experimental inoculations of donkeys and guinea-pigs produced negative results.

Encysted parasites were recognized in many of these nodules, and it was concluded that they were in most cases possibly due to some parasite, *e.g.*, echinococcus, sclerostomum, etc.

Calcareous nodules were also occasionally found in the liver and spleen ; these were also frequently examined and experimented with, but as glanders was in no case proved, or detected, it was concluded they were due to other causes, *e.g.*, of vegetable or parasitic origin.

Diagnosis

Under this heading I don't think that I can do better than quoting first Nocard and Leclainche, who state that the ulcer of epizootic lymphangitis is frequently typical, and is characterized by its exuberant granulations, its bright red colour, its inverted edges, and its thick creamy discharge of pus, in fact the appearances are all quite different from those of glanders, although in old cases they are less characteristic.

However, as long as any doubt exists as to the correct diagnosis, it is advisable to have recourse to all the available experimental methods in order to arrive at an undisputable conclusion.

Examination of the pus gives a certain and immediate diagnosis. The cryptococcus is said to be easily seen without staining with a magnifying power of 400 to 500 diameters, but personally I like a power of not less than 800 diameters for unstained specimens ; the organism is recognized by its size, shape, and highly refractory double outline.

The parasites are almost as easy to find in a scraping of mucous membrane or tissue, but are generally not so numerous there as in material from a fresh pustule.

Careful mallein testing should in no case be followed by a re-action, except when glanders is co-existent.

An inclination to heal will be noticed in some of the pustules and sores, especially when energetic treatment is resorted to.

In the event of suspicious indolent subcutaneous nodules being observed, diagnosis might be accelerated by extirpation and microscopical examination of sections and smears from the nodules. However, I have no knowledge of this method of diagnosis having yet been carried out, although in dealing with an outbreak I have frequently had resort to removing such suspicious nodules by complete extirpation as a precautionary measure. At the same time, one must remember that in dealing with an outbreak every effort should be made to reduce the number of wounds to a minimum, so in adopting this as a method of diagnosis there are many points which require very careful consideration before it could be generally recommended.

Differential Diagnosis

1. *Glanders* (farcy), as has been already inferred, is the disease with which epizootic lymphangitis is most likely to be confounded, and the latter may be distinguished from it (glanders) by the following points :—

(i) Healthy appearance of the animal generally. Emaciation and unthriftiness being only present in very advanced cases in which the disease tends to become generalized.

D

(ii) Almost invariable absence of fever.

(iii) Unimpaired appetite.

(iv) Characteristic appearance of the ulcers and sores, which have an inclination to granulate and with energetic treatment to heal, and further, in some cases to heal with practically no treatment.

(v) The whitish colour and thick creamy consistency of the pus.

(vi) The benign and curable character of the disease.

(vii) Non-reaction to mallein.

(viii) Inconstancy of submaxillary glandular enlargement, even in the cases when the nasal mucous membranes are the seat of the disease, and the fact that even when the submaxillary glands are enlarged they are not necessarily fixed to the jaw—a symptom which is generally accepted to be invariably present in glanders, although personally I have come to the conclusion that such a condition is not constant in glanders either.

(ix) In the nasal variety, the ulcerations in glanders are generally more extensive and, in most cases, spread from above downwards, whereas, in this disease, the ulcerations are generally less extensive, and are more frequently found in the lower third of the nasal chambers with a tendency to spread upwards; the discharge is less copious, and is not in proportion to the lesions found on the membranes.

(x) The invariable presence of cryptococcus in the pus and tissues, its size, characteristic appearance and staining.

(xi) Glanders (farcy) not supervening after experimental inoculation of donkeys, guinea-pigs, horses, and other susceptible animals.

(xii) The appearance of the culture.

(xiii) The *post-mortem* appearances.

(xiv) The application of the serum test.

2. *Ulcerative lymphangitis.* This is a disease which has been differentiated from the other forms of lymphangitis by Nocard, and is due to a bacillus discovered by him in 1892, and care should be taken not to confound it with the disease herein described, as has already been done by many writers on the subject.

As far as I can gather from the literature on the subject, it is a disease that has only been recognized in France, although Nocard and Leclainche have a footnote in their book referring to Moore's cases as possibly simulating the disease ; but judging from Pease's pamphlet on the subject, I am inclined to think that they were none other than epizootic lymphangitis, as the cases did not easily yield to treatment, and experimental inoculations made from them failed to produce orchitis in guinea-pigs, a point which is said to be characteristic of the ulcerative form of lymphangitis.

Schwarzkoff, in an article in the *American Veterinary Review*, describes some cases occurring amongst the American horses during the campaign in the Philippines under the name of tropical ulcers of the horse, which Nocard and Leclainche also refer to ; the cases were noticed during the rainy season, and may possibly have been nothing more than *bursatti*, or a vesicular eruption around the coronets, as is often seen amongst horses running at grass during the rainy season in India. According to Nocard and Leclainche, the bacillus of ulcerative lymphangitis is found abundantly in the pus, it is an ordinary saprophyte, and is easily stained by Gram's method.

In this disease the sores are also said to resemble very much those of farcy, but there is an absence of induration of the lymphatic glands, and the ulcers and sores easily yield to treatment. Experimental inoculation into the peritoneal cavity of the guinea-pig produces orchitis in six to eight days, similar to that obtained in glanders and, for that reason, may lead to confusion; however, the question is easily solved by resorting to the mallein test, and also to the use of other experimental animals, *e.g.*, donkeys. The inoculated guinea-pig very seldom succumbs to the disease, but it is not uncommon for one of the testicles to be almost entirely destroyed; in ordinary subcutaneous inoculation a large abscess forms in four or five days, and the adjacent lymphatics become invaded.

Experimental subcutaneous inoculation of a horse, mule, or donkey produces an abscess in six to ten days. Inoculation with a culture of the organism kills a guinea-pig in twenty-four to forty-eight hours. Rabbits resist an intraperitoneal injection of a culture. White mice are killed in twenty-four to forty-eight hours, and a culture of the bacillus can be generally obtained from the blood. Pigeons sometimes die four to six days after an intravenous inoculation, but fowls are refractory.

The organism has very little resistance and is destroyed at a temperature of $56°$ C. in one hour, and at $65°$ C. in less than a quarter of an hour. And, contrary to the epizootic form, the treatment is simple—the disease is less indolent—and if experimental inoculation and mallein testing is resorted to there should be no difficulty in the diagnosis.

3. *Simple lymphangitis and its sequelae, i.e., suppurative lymphangitis*, due to acute inflammation and septic infection, is differentiated from epizootic lymphangitis by the absence of the characteristic symptoms and of the cryptococcus, and the presence of various other organisms, particularly staphylococci, the streptococcus brevis, and occasionally the bacillus necrosis. This disease is invariably easily amenable to treatment, except when synovial bursa and joints become involved, but if the case is at all indolent it is advisable, as a precautionary measure, to examine specimens from the discharges under the microscope in order to ascertain as soon as possible what is actually retarding the healing process.

4. *Tubercular Lymphangitis.* Attention to the similarity of this disease and epizootic lymphangitis was brought to the notice of the members of the National Veterinary Association at their recent meeting by Professor Mettam, who exhibited an excellent lantern slide showing tubercular lesions on the right fore-arm of an ox. The clinical symptoms would appear to have been almost identical with those seen in Plate VI of this work, and a correct diagnosis was only arrived at by the demonstration of tubercle bacillus and the absence of the saccharomyces.

5. *Bursatti.* This has already been referred to, and is a disease seen principally in tropical climates, especially during the rainy seasons. It is well known in India and Burmah, and in the United States of America, where it is known under the name of *Leeches.* Cases are also reported to have been noticed in France. The disease is due to the presence of a form of mycelium not yet classified, and is characterized by the appearance of multiple granulating fistulous sores, which do not suppurate but are accompanied by well

defined tumefaction of the subcutaneous tissues immediately surrounding them, and by the formation of
peculiar hard concretions in the centre of the wounds;
the latter have little tendency to heal until the
concretions, or *kunkar* as they are commonly called in
India, have been completely removed, and the wound
treated with strong escharotics and antiseptics.

Horses and mules are the principal animals
affected, but cattle are also said to contract the disease.
Should two or more bursatti sores make their appearance, particularly on a limb on the course of the
lymphatics, as they may do, as a sequel to ordinary
suppurative lymphangitis, they may give rise to
suspicions of epizootic lymphangitis, but with the
various means now to hand and the almost invariable
presence of the concretions, there should be no difficulty
in arriving at an accurate diagnosis.

6. *Botryomycosis* is a disease due to the presence
of the *Botryomyces equi*, which get into the tissues and
bring about the formation of numerous subcutaneous
fibrous tumours, often seen under the saddle and collar.
However, they are easily differentiated by the absence of
cording, the fibrous appearance of the nodules, and
by the presence of the specific organism, which is easily
stained with aniline dyes, notably Loeffler's blue.

7. *The other diseases*, which may be confounded
with epizootic lymphangitis, are practically all those
which are mentioned in the differential diagnosis for
glanders, namely, strangles, and its sequelae, variola
equina, follicular ulceration, stomatitis contagiosa pus-
tulosa, injuries of the nasal mucous membrane, carcino-
mata, sarcomata, actinomycosis, melanosis, and other
new growths, such as subcutaneous fibrous tumours,
warts, etc. : parasitic diseases, especially those affecting
the nasal cavity, urticaria, petechial fever, acne contagiosa,

vesicular eruptions on the genitals and dourine. However, these diseases should be all easily diagnosed by their characteristics, together with the presence of their own particular organisms, if due to such, and the constant absence of the characteristic symptoms of epizootic lymphangitis and of the cryptococcus.

EXPERIMENTAL INOCULATION AND SUSCEPTIBLE SPECIES

The disease is common to horses, mules, and donkeys. Nocard and Leclainche state that mules are more susceptible than horses, but my experience is that, given the conditions the same, the susceptibility of horses and mules is about equal, and both are probably more susceptible than donkeys.

Tokishige's experiments go to prove that the disease may also affect cattle, but I am inclined to think that this requires further corroboration, although he states that he verified his diagnosis by the presence of a form of saccharomyces. His experiments with guinea-pigs were in some cases complicated with glanders, so are not conclusive, but he failed to reproduce the disease in rats, hares, pigs, dogs, and cats.

Haubert, Delrade, and Wiart's attempts to reproduce the disease in horses failed. Tixier, Delamotte, Chauvrat, and Peuch reproduced the disease in donkeys. Nocard reproduced it in horses, mules, and donkeys, but failed in cattle, goats, and guinea-pigs. Rivolta and Micellone succeeded in horses, as also did Bassi and Venuta, but they failed in goats. Moore appears to have succeeded in a horse and failed in guinea-pigs. Lingard carried out experimental inoculations on various species of animals in India, but I am not aware of his final results.

Personally, I reproduced the disease in horses, mules, and donkeys, but failed in cattle, sheep, goats, and guinea-pigs, all the usual methods of experimental inoculation being resorted to, but the best results were obtained from the inoculation of ordinary wounds. In all cases attempts to reproduce the disease by ingestion were followed by negative results.

Recently Mettam reproduced the disease in a horse at the Royal Veterinary College of Ireland, Dublin, but also failed in the ox, using the same material.

The inoculations made by the various investigators of this disease were carried out in the following different methods, viz. :—scarification, artificial inoculation of wounds and mucous membranes, subcutaneous inoculations, and by ingestion. All the methods mentioned, except the latter, appear to have been attended with more or less success in the susceptible species, but the results show that infection is really rather difficult, and may at times fail to reproduce the disease even in susceptible animals, or it may only show itself after a long time.

In my experiments carried out in India, the first symptom observed, after a subcutaneous inoculation on the side of a donkey's neck (simultaneous inoculations having been also made in both nostrils by scarification), was a small, round, hard, slightly painful enlargement about the size of a hazel nut at the seat of inoculation on the neck after thirty-two days ; this remained much the same for about a week, except that the painfulness gradually subsided, and there was a slight inclination for the swelling to decrease.

On the forty-fifth day the enlargement increased to three times its previous size, and it became softer and more painful. On the forty-eight day it returned to its original size. On the fifty-third day a small vesicle was noticed to have broken out on the edge of the near nostril, leaving a minute ulcer, on a scar resulting from scarification, just where the skin adjoins the nasal mucous membrane. On the fifty-fourth day the ulcer on the edge of the off nostril had increased in size, and was discharging slightly. Two small ulcers had now developed at the edge of the off nostril, one of which was almost on the mucous membrane itself. At the same time the enlargement at the seat of inoculation on the neck had become partially divided into two small nodules, one of which was softening and preparing to form into a pustule.

On the fifty-eighth day a small chain of vesicles had broken out along the scar on the edge of the near nostril, and a pustule had now formed at the site of inoculation on the neck.

On the sixty-seventh day the enlargement on the near side of neck had increased, the pustule had burst, and was discharging a thick yellow pus; the small ulcers on the edge of both nostrils were increasing in size.

On the sixty-ninth day a corded lymphatic had now developed on the near side of the neck, running downwards from the pustule.

On the seventy-fourth day several corded lymphatics were radiating from the sore which had now formed on the neck, and several other pustules were rapidly developing along their course. There was also a good deal of discharge from the wound; and the ulcerating sores on the edges of both nostrils were increasing in size and beginning to coalesce. The case having first been tested with mallein, and, giving no reaction, was now destroyed. The *post-mortem* examination revealed that the internal organs were healthy, and no further lesions of the disease other than those already described were present.

It occasionally happens that attempts to reproduce the disease are only followed by one or more subcutaneous indolent nodules, which, after fluctuating up and down for some weeks or months, finally disappear, leaving no sign of the disease. These conditions are no doubt brought about by the active resistance of the tissues, and the effect of phagocytes. Nocard and Leclainche state that considerable resistance is made by the tissues, and that phagocytosis is very active—that the cryptococci which penetrate beyond the lymph glands are attacked and nearly all destroyed by the leucocytes, but that occasionally the organisms get into the circulation and set up specific lesions in the lungs.

A man is reported to have inoculated himself with the disease (in the arm) during the early part of an outbreak which occurred in Bangalore, India, in 1899. I regret that I am not in possession of the facts of this case, but I understand that all the symptoms became well developed, numerous bubos formed along the course of the lymphatics, right up to the arm pit, and that after suffering pretty severely from the disease for several weeks a cure was effected.

Another case is reported from South Africa, where a man attempted to inoculate himself, but failed. Personally I have conducted both the surgical treatment and *post-mortem* examinations of several hundred animals affected with the disease, under various conditions, and have from time to time run considerable risk of becoming inoculated, but have so far escaped the disease.

Busse in 1895 observed a saccharomyces analogous to the cryptococcus of Rivolta in a sarcomatous growth on the tibia of a woman, but the further investigation of the case tends to prove that this was some other organism.

However, although to my knowledge there is no authentic information forthcoming of a human being ever becoming infected with the disease, and that accidental inoculation appears to be unlikely, I think that until something more definite is known about it the risk of man contracting the disease is, although remote, always to be carefully considered and guarded against in dealing with this disease.

RESISTANCE OF THE VIRUS

According to Rivolta and Micellone, it may be destroyed in a few minutes at a temperature of 80° C., but that it resists the action of a 5 per cent. solution of carbolic acid. My own experience is, that in the treatment of the cases, carbolic acid is practically useless, and that the only thing that can be relied on to destroy the organism is perchloride of mercury, and of this a solution of not less than 1 in 250 is recommended.

IMMUNITY

Tokishige states that in Japan the popular idea amongst farmers and quacks is that one attack reduces the predisposition of the animal to the disease, but he himself says that this is questionable and requires further investigation.

Peuch, in writing of African farcy and, no doubt, referring to this disease, states that the predisposition is diminished after one attack, but most other writers on the subject have seldom omitted to point out the likelihood of the disease recurring.

I have personal experience of several cases breaking out again after they had been apparently cured, but must point out that, in all these cases, the disease

developed at the same place in which the original
lesions were present, and in these cases I was of the
opinion that the organisms had simply become inert for
the time being, as a result of so many of them being
removed or destroyed by the treatment, and that gradually
they began to increase and became active again. I do not
think that reinfection from external sources was the
cause of their recrudescence, but that simply the cure,
in the first instance, was incomplete, *i.e.*, all the organisms
were not either removed or destroyed, and Nocard and
Leclainche point out that a relapse is to be feared, for
a long time, from small abscesses containing the
organisms, remaining in the cicatrized tissues, which,
breaking out, become a fresh source of infection.

Predisposing Causes

On this point opinions seem to differ.

Tokishige states that the most cases occur in
animals between the age of three and four years, and
that it prevails more in low marshy districts than in
mountainous localities, more in rainy seasons than in
dry, and more in cold weather than in hot, but that the
latter is accounted for by the fact that in Japan the
animals are crowded into stables during the winter ;
wounds and contusions are more frequent as a result,
and the modes of infection are, therefore, much easier
under these circumstances. On the other hand, Lingard
goes so far as to say that the disease cannot exist in cold
countries, and mentions that experiments conducted at
Muktesar, India, have shown that a cure can be effected
by removing animals to a high level, *i.e.*, 7,500 feet,
and recommends it as a method of accelerating a cure.
Head, writing recently in the *Veterinary Record*, states
that he had over one hundred patients at one time

suffering from the disease in South Africa, and mentions that 'a change of air to a high district helps the case.'

My own experience is that neither climates, districts, nor seasons have themselves practically anything to do with the spread and development of the disease, although indirectly they may, as the various conditions, which are subject to and altered by them, may aid or retard development, and on reference to the history and geographical distribution of the disease, it will be found that these opinions are fairly well substantiated.

General Methods of Infection

The infection may be carried by or on anything— e.g., vehicles, soil, fences, dust, gates, stables, harness, horse clothing, grooming and stable utensils, litter, fodder, parasites, flies, etc. ; by attendants, and more particularly by amateur and careless veterinary assistants and even surgeons—on their hands, clothes, or on sponges, tow, cotton-wool, bandages, bottles and other pharmacy utensils, twitches, instruments, necessaries, wound dressings, etc. A few cases may infect themselves by contact, or, what is commoner, they may infect themselves in one or more places additional to that of the original seat of the disease, more especially on the lips or mucous membrane of the nose and eyes— by rubbing and biting, and in these cases generally accidentally, in their attempts to remove flies from a wound on themselves which is already the seat of the disease.

Cases affecting the conjunctiva, with no external symptom, save a slight discharge which passes unnoticed for days, weeks, and even months, are most prolific in spreading the disease, particularly in India, where the native attendants go from horse to horse with dirty little cloths (called *jarhans*) wiping the horses' eyes and noses and infecting them as they go along—in fact, I attributed the spread of the disease, in one outbreak which I had to deal with, to this same cause. As infection, apparently, only takes place by the inoculation of wounds, all those conditions which predispose animals to wounds and abrasions also as a matter of course predispose to the development and spread of the disease. Therefore, transmission is facilitated by the herding and co-habitation of animals, and this explains why the disease is especially associated with army horses, more particularly in remount depôts, and also amongst horses belonging to large companies. Anything that retards the healing of wounds also predisposes to the spread of the disease, and this fact, no doubt, accounts for the disease being more prevalent in warm climates, particularly in the rainy season, and in low-lying and inundated districts, where flies are very numerous, and where the healing of wounds is protracted by exuberant granulations with a tendency to bursatti. Therefore, the removal of animals to an elevation has the advantage of removing those difficulties in combating the disease, and bears out the observations of other writers on the subject. Experiments carried out in India proved that the source of infection may be in the soil, *e.g.*, mud from stable floors, some considerable time after the patient had been removed from the stable.

TREATMENT

The great secret of success is an early diagnosis and a thorough understanding of the disease. Destruction of the virus is the first object to be obtained, and this having been accomplished, the parts recently affected will rapidly heal.

External Treatment

In slight cases, complete extirpation of the tissues invaded, followed by the application of the actual cautery and antiseptic dressing, is generally to be recommended and considered practical, although in some few cases very good results have been obtained without these drastic surgical methods, which are, however, more particularly recommended by French veterinary surgeons. The risk of re-infection during operating and the blemishes which remain are the great drawbacks to this treatment, so that I am inclined to recommend the simpler treatment of carefully lancing each pustule when ripe, and using the hot iron, in the form of small budding irons, together with internal treatment, in preference to extensive surgical treatment. Once cording of the lymphatics has developed, the case is much more difficult to deal with. If, however, the cording is localized and well defined, it may be possible to have recourse to complete extirpation ; the *modus operandi* is as follows :—Cut down on to the lymphatic vessel, and divide it with the actual cautery a few inches above the termination of the cording; the affected portion of the vessel is then dissected out and removed complete, with the tissues and foci from which the disease is developing ; after which the operation wound is thoroughly cauterized and treated with antiseptics as in the first case.

In cases where there is diffuse swelling and chronic thickening, surgical intervention is much more difficult and less likely to be attended with success. However, beginning from the periphery, all the affected lymphatic cords should be laid open and treated as above described, all abscesses and pustules should be lanced, their cavities then thoroughly scraped out and afterwards treated with the actual cautery and antiseptic dressing.

When operation is decided upon, it must be carried out thoroughly, and under strict aseptic precautions, great care being necessary to avoid re-infection through the operation wound.

Almost every antiseptic and escharotic has been used in the treatment of the disease, and of those generally used I recommend corrosive sublimate in strong solutions, not less than 1-250.

The application of a good strong blister of bin-iodide of mercury is recommended to some cases, as it tends to bring the abscesses and pustules to a head, and so facilitates treatment.

Great care must be taken that wounds are not being re-infected by flies, dressings, etc., or that the patient does not bite them, or rub his nose or eyes in them.

INTERNAL TREATMENT

In this I recommend administrating compounds of iodine and mercury, both of which seem to have a more or less specific effect on the disease, particularly the mercury.

Corrosive sublimate in doses of half to one grain, in solution or put in the drinking water, or bin-iodide of mercury in doses of three to ten grains daily, in powder placed on the tongue.

A dose of physic should be administered at the outset, the patient kept on soft feeding and given a little Epsom salts periodically if thought necessary.

MORTALITY AND PROGNOSIS

From statistics the average mortality is about ten to fifteen per cent., and under favourable conditions the prognosis is invariably favourable, provided that the case has not been allowed to run too far before proper treatment is taken in hand. I always look upon the prognosis as unfavourable when proper means for isolation, and strictly aseptic arrangements for energetic treatment, and an intelligent dependable attendant are not available.

The prognosis of cases in which the nasal mucous membrane, conjunctiva, scrotum and sheath (after castration), joints or sheaths of tendons are affected, is generally most unfavourable, particularly those in which the mucous membranes are the seat of the disease. As it is most difficult to ascertain the extent of the disease, the delicate membranes attacked will not stand the severe treatment required, and finally it is practically impossible to know for certain when such a case is absolutely cured of the disease. Therefore very great risk to the well-being of the community is incurred by keeping such cases under treatment ; in fact, unless the most thorough and complete arrangements exist for isolation and treatment, immediate destruction of all verified cases is recommended, particularly where large numbers of horses are being dealt with. But again, even these stringent measures are not followed by the success anticipated, unless every detail of the prophylactic measures are most strictly adhered to and intelligently carried out.

Under the most favourable circumstances, the time required to effect a cure may vary from one month to six or more according to the extent the disease has developed and class of case being dealt with.

Prophylaxis

1. In the stamping out of outbreaks and the prevention of this disease, it is imperative that the

E

veterinary surgeon employed should have a thorough knowledge of the disease. He should be thoroughly acquainted with the appearance of the organism under the microscope, and he should be able to examine pus and scrapings from suspicious wounds himself, so that his diagnosis should be, in every case, quick and absolutely accurate. Failing this, a specialist on the disease should be employed to investigate the outbreak, and assist the veterinary surgeon in charge, and at his inspections, pus and scrapings from every wound, no matter how slight, should be examined under the microscope ; and during his absence, specimens, *i.e.*, smears on slides or cover-glass preparations from any other suspicious cases which occur, should be forwarded to him for examination without delay.

2. In a unit or stud, in which the disease has been recognized, daily inspection of every animal should be most carefully carried out, and at these inspections the whole body should be carefully examined, especially those regions which are most exposed to galls, wounds (kicks), and contusions. The mucous membranes and submaxillary glands should be examined as for glanders, and if there is any symptom of conjunctivitis or discharge from the eyes, the conjunctivae should be inverted and thoroughly examined ; in fact, in any case this detail should be periodically carried out. All old scars and subcutaneous enlargements should be carefully noted and watched. The most susceptible regions should be carefully handled for symptoms of corded lymphatics, and for this a touch acquired by a practical knowledge of the disease is a great advantage in diagnosis. In the inspection of large numbers of horses, it is a great advantage to have two veterinary surgeons working together, one on either side of the horse, the horses being brought out of the stables and

led up one by one, and walked quietly back to their stall.

3. The men, and those who are in charge of the animals, should be carefully instructed in the rudimentary symptoms of the disease, and they should also be instructed to immediately point out any animal developing swellings, nodules, wounds, or sores, no matter how trifling they appear to be, or from what they have been due.

4. The use of sponges, both for grooming purposes, and for dressing wounds, etc., in a hospital should be discontinued, as also should the small rubbers used in India, especially for wiping horses' noses and eyes.

5. All animals recognized as affected with the disease should be immediately isolated for treatment, or destroyed and cremated, as the case may be. All suspicious animals should be isolated separately from the others until such time as may be required to accurately diagnose whether they are free from disease or not, and then treated accordingly.

6. In an outbreak, even after the organism has been recognized, should any case present symptoms suspicious of glanders, recourse should be had to mallein testing and any other means of diagnosis thought necessary ; in case both diseases should prove to be co-existing in the one animal, in which case the combined prophylactic measures for the stamping out of both diseases must be carried out.

7. Every effort should be made to reduce the number of wounds, galls, and other predisposing causes of the spread of the disease to a minimum.

8. The system of having wound dressings in the hands of amateurs, and also those of shoeing smiths, farriers, and others, for treating slight cases in the lines,

as has been the custom in our army, as well as that of many continental powers, should be discontinued.

9. In the treatment of wounds the strictest asepsis should be observed. Most small wounds and abrasions are best left alone, and those that require treatment should be sent to the hospital, where they should be first thoroughly cleansed with clean cold water from a stand pipe. The use of tow and cotton wool should be restricted as much as possible, and when required a fresh piece should be used for each wound, and afterwards immediately disposed of by burning. All wounds should be then dressed with a solution of perchloride of mercury, strength not to be less than 1-500, applied with a glass syringe, the nozzle of which should not be allowed to touch the wound. A little boric powder or iodoform should then be dusted over it with an insufflator, great care being also taken that the nozzle of the insufflator does not touch the wound, which, if thought necessary, is covered with a clean piece of cotton wool and a clean linen bandage. In the dressing of wounds great care should be taken not to infect the mouth of the bottle containing the antiseptic solution by placing tow or cotton against it in order to saturate them with the solution, but a glazed gallipot or such like receptacle should be used for decanting as much solution as may be required to dress just one wound, after which any that remains should be thrown away, and the receptacle thoroughly cleaned. Anything which goes towards reducing the risk of infection is also recommended; therefore all wounds should be covered up either by cotton wool and bandaging, or what is often much better, gauze. Disinfectants should be freely used in the stables, which must, together with their surroundings, be kept clean and free from smell; fly papers may be also used with advantage when thought practical.

10.   Harness and saddlery used on infected cases should be thoroughly disinfected with perchloride of mercury solution 1-250, as far as it is practical, or else they should be destroyed altogether, *i.e.*, burnt with the carcase, together with the litter, grooming kit, and clothing, all of which should invariably also be destroyed. The clothing of attendants on infected animals should be thoroughly disinfected, if not burnt.

Periodical disinfection of all the other animals' grooming kits, stable utensils, etc., is also recommended.

11.   The stables occupied by infected animals should be thoroughly disinfected.   The walls, wood-work, and mangers first singed, then washed down and scrubbed with perchloride of mercury solution, the floorings being swilled out with it at the same time, after which the walls are washed with quicklime, the woodwork is painted, and the floorings sprinkled with quicklime.   Should the floors consist of mud or other permeable material, it is advisable to burn litter over it, and then remove at least three to six inches off the surface and renew it with fresh material ; the portion removed being well mixed with quicklime is buried six feet in the ground, and, if possible, in some waste place where permeation is least likely to take place.

12.   In a stud where an outbreak has occurred it should be considered infected until at least six months have elapsed from the date on which the last case was either separated from the healthy horses or discharged cured when treatment has been adopted ; further, the horses of the stud should be kept under observation (*i.e.*, their movements carefully reported, so that they are not lost sight of) for another six months.

13.   In dealing with outbreaks of this disease it is advisable to extirpate all suspicious indolent sub-cutaneous nodules, whether the animal is known to

have the disease or not, as they may possibly contain the cryptococcus. Having recourse to this method has the advantage of greatly reducing the number of animals under observation, and does away with a great deal of unnecessary isolation of many horses which are free from the disease.

14. When the disease makes its appearance in a large stud farm or remount depôt, where young stock have been running out, it is advisable to have all the animals taken up, and either put in stables or picketed out in batches of about fifty to one hundred, each animal being well clear of the other, so that they cannot kick or bite one another, and issues should only be made from batches which have been for at least six to twelve months clear. All the animals should, after due quarantine, be issued from the stud, and the stables should then be all thoroughly disinfected as already mentioned, the land should be dressed with quicklime, which may be either left to penetrate itself when the rain comes, or be ploughed in and the land then cropped. Even allowing it to run to meadow and then burning it standing, as can easily be done in a country like India, may also be resorted to. If none of these measures are adopted, cattle should be run on it for a year before being re-opened for horses, mules, or donkeys.

15. Finally, the free use of the microscope cannot be too forcibly impressed upon those who may have to deal with an outbreak of this disease. Much time and unnecessary isolation of animals is saved by an early diagnosis, such as can only be made by the microscope. Material from suspicious wounds should be periodically examined, and even in cases when nothing has been detected at first, further examination may prove the presence of the organisms.

Concluding Remarks

As there seems to be some difference of opinion as to the advisability of undertaking the treatment of cases of this disease, and also some doubt as to effectiveness of the prophylactic measures recommended herein, I am giving some statistics in connexion with the last outbreak of this disease which I had practically sole charge of, at least, from the diagnosis of the first case up to a couple of weeks after the last case had been recognized and separated from the healthy horses.

The outbreak, as will be seen, began, or at least was first detected, on the 13th May, 1902, and was amongst the horses of a cavalry regiment in India —strength about 500 horses—the source of infection was never satisfactorily decided. The measures taken for dealing with it were drawn up by the author. They were similar to those which I have detailed in the foregoing pages, and the success in stamping out the outbreak was considered to be due to (1) Previous experience and knowledge of the disease. (2) Early diagnosis in every case. (3) Facilities for thorough isolation and treatment. (4) Thoroughness with which the prophylactic measures were carried out.

I might mention that the cured cases were allowed to return to the lines within one month of being discharged, that the regiment proceeded on manoeuvres shortly afterwards, and that no cases have occurred in this unit since. However, unless one is quite certain that such cases are going to be under your own eye for some considerable time, it is most advisable to adhere to the six months' isolation previously recommended as a minimum, especially where large studs and remounts depôts are concerned.

STATISTICS OF AN OUTBREAK OF EPIZOOTIC LYMPHANGITIS AMONGST THE HORSES OF A CAVALRY REGIMENT IN INDIA, 1902

No.	Symptoms and Seat of the Lesions	Admitted	Discharged	Cured	Destroyed	Died	Remarks
1	Ulcers both nostrils and discharge from the same, submaxillary glands enlarged, subcutaneous nodules all over body, legs swelled all round, fever, etc. ...	13-5-02	23-5-02	—	1	—	Disease became acute and generalized. Case from which Plates XIV, XV, and XVI were taken.
2	Ulcerations and granulation on the mucous membrane, near side nostril ...	19-5-02	15-10-02	—	1	—	Originally only a very slight abrasion on the membrane.
3	Granulations on mucous membranes both sides nostrils ...	27-5-02	9-10-02	—	1	—	Mucous membrane very much thickened in this case.
4	Granulating sore on muzzle ...	29-5-02	15-10-02	—	1	—	Very similar to the case from which Plate V was taken.
5	Enlarged near hind leg; seat of infection, near hind heel ...	3-6-02	23-8-02	1	—	—	Original wound caused by a rope-gall.
6	Conjunctivitis near eye, submaxillary glands enlarged, clinical symptoms near fore-arm and shoulder ...	6-6-02	21-8-02	—	—	1	Similar to a combination of the cases from which Plates VI and XVII were taken, and, like case No. I, the disease became acute and generalized.
7	Granulating wound near side jaw ...	7-6-02	19-7-02	1	—	—	A slight case.
8	Chain of pustules on back and loins ...	24-6-02	23-8-02	1	—	—	A slight case.
9	Chain of subcutaneous nodules near side girth ...	24-6-02	19-7-02	1	—	—	The nodules in this case were small and never came to a head, but gradually disappeared.
10	Chain of subcutaneous nodules near side loins and hip ...	28-6-02	19-7-02	1	—	—	Similar to case No. 9.
11	Abscess off-side rib, originally appeared to be the seat of a small punctured wound	29-7-02	16-10-02	1	—	—	A comparatively slight case.
Totals		11	11	6	4	1	

Note.—In addition to the above some twenty-eight horses came under observation for periods varying from three days to a month.

The percentage of mucous membrane (unfavourable, see p. 47) cases in this outbreak is much above the average, and was, most probably, due to circumstances peculiar to horse management in India (see p. 44) where the attendants are continually wiping the horses' eyes and noses with dirty little cloths, and more especially in the hot weather when dust storms are frequent and flies are troublesome.

With the exception of cases Nos. 9 and 10, from which no material was obtainable, the diagnosis of all the above cases was verified by microscopical examination.

The disease having been recently scheduled under the Diseases of Animals Acts in Great Britain and Ireland, I am including the orders of the Board of Agriculture on the subject, *vide* appendix.

THE END

PLATE 1

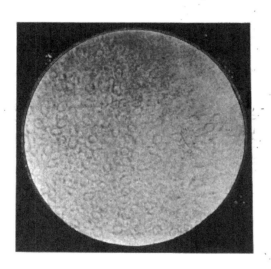

Saccharomyces from an abscess (Zeiss Ocul, 4 object, J. Immers).
From a micro-photograph prepared by Tokishige and
Dr. Okura

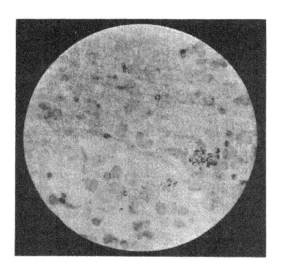

From a micro-photograph prepared by the author from a specimen prepared and stained by Professor A. E. Mettam at the Royal Veterinary College of Ireland, showing a group of saccharomyces clumped together, and also several characteristic saccharomyces in various parts of the field, and a large number of pus organisms which have also taken up the stain.　×　800 diameters.

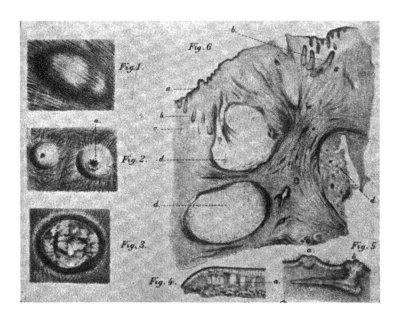

Figs. 1 to 5 are from drawings by Tanaka.   Fig. 6 is from a drawing by Tokishige.

Fig. 1, subcutaneous node ; Fig. 2, cutaneous nodes with crater-like opening *a* ; Fig. 3, fungoid
ulcer ; Fig. 4, saccharomycotic changes in hair follicles and in the corresponding subcutis ;
Fig. 5, transection through cutaneous nodules, *a*, natural size ; Fig. 6, section
of skin (picro carmine prep. ; zeiss ocul. 2, object A), *a*, epidermis,
bb, hair follicles, *c*, sebaceous gland, *ddd*, saccharomycotic
herds in the thickened skin and subcutis.

PLATE IV

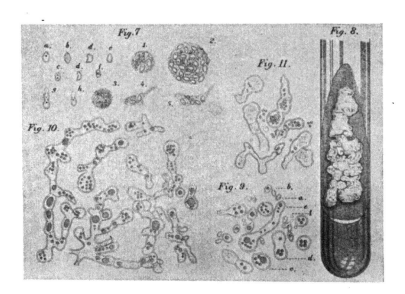

From a drawing by Tokishige.

Fig. 7, different forms of saccharomyces; ; *a* monogranulated, *b* with finely granulated contents, *c* with two granules, *dd* semilunar form, *e* apparently empty, *f* with larger granule, *g* three cells conjoined, *h* with bud-like appendix ; 1-2 pus corpuscles containing many saccharomyces, 3 the same with granules, 4-5 connective tissue corpuscles with saccharomyces.

Fig. 8, colony of saccharomyces on glycerine agar (about seven months old).

Fig. 9, vegetative form after a fortnight, *a* original, *b* swollen, *c* spherical form with a number of granules, *d* dumb-bell form, *e* young hyphen, *f* extracellular granule.

Fig. 10, the same two months old.   Fig. 11, the same more than one year old.

PLATE V

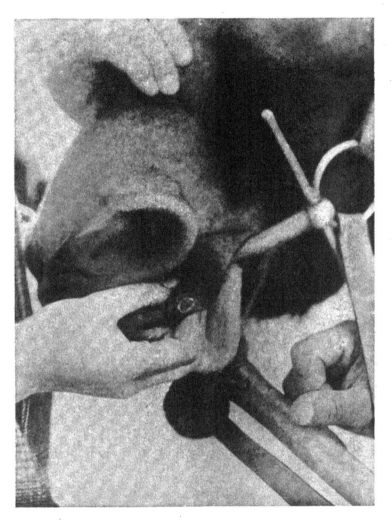

Shows a small typical granulating sore infected with the disease on the lip of a mule.
From a photograph taken in India.   Diagnosis verified by microscopical
examination for Mallein testing.

PLATE VI

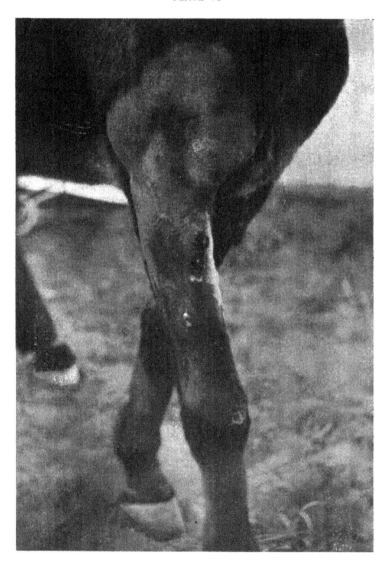

Shows the disease in an Indian country-bred mule, extending from the off knee (the
seat of infection) winding up forearm to anti-brachial region. From a
photograph taken in India. Diagnosis verified by microscopical
examination and Mallein testing.

PLATE VII

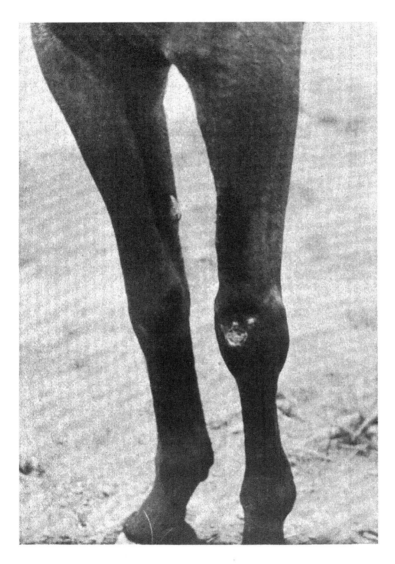

Shows the disease in an Indian country-bred horse, extending from the knee (the original seat of infection) up fore-arm to anti-brachial region, as seen in Plate VIII, the continuation of the lesions in the same animal.   Diagnosis verified by microscopical examination and mallein testin:.

PLATE VIII

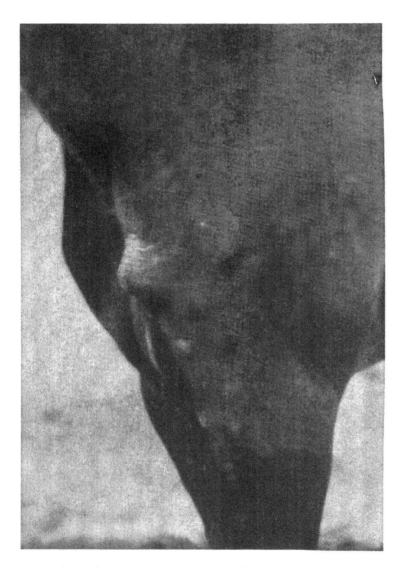

From a photograph of the same case as Plate VII. Showing nodules in the anti-brachial region varying from the size of a pigeon's to a hen's egg.

PLATE IX

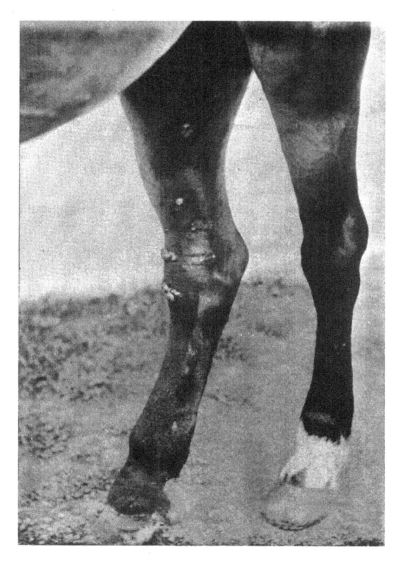

Shows the disease in an Australian mare. Affecting the off hind leg, as seen from the
near side—infection having taken place from a cracked heel, extending up and
winding round the leg to groin, pustules having broken out in front of the
hock and inside of the tibia. From a photograph taken in India.
Diagnosis verified by microscopical examination.

PLATE X

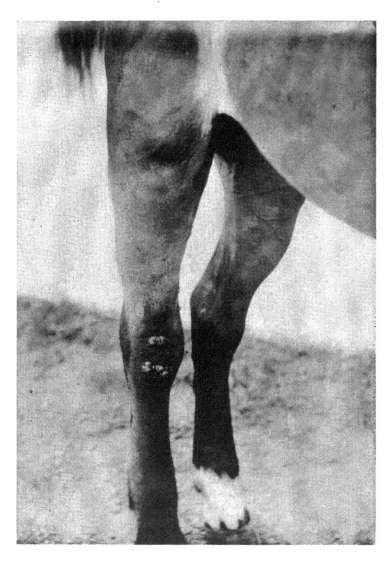

Same case as Plate IX, only as seen from the off side.

PLATE XI

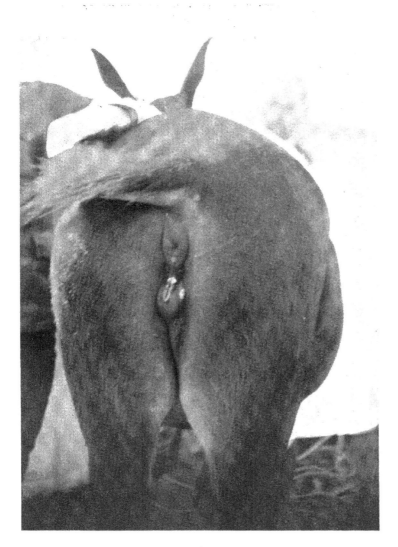

Shows the disease in an Indian country-bred mule. Extending from the edge of the vulva
(the seat of the infection and originally only a small scratch) to the perinaeum, and
mammary gland. From a photograph taken in India. Diagnosis
verified by microscopical examination and mallein testing.

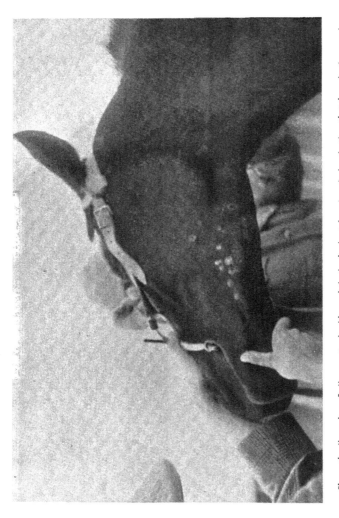

Shows the disease in an Indian country-bred horse, infection having taken place during the time that the animal was under treatment for strangles some weeks previously; the case was cured, and the lesions seen now, developed later. All the tissues in the submaxillary space being more or less affected, multiple pustules formed, and the disease also spread round the jaw, across the face, Steno's duct also becoming the seat of an abscess. From a photograph taken in India. Diagnosis verified by microscopical examination and mallein testing.

PLATE XIII

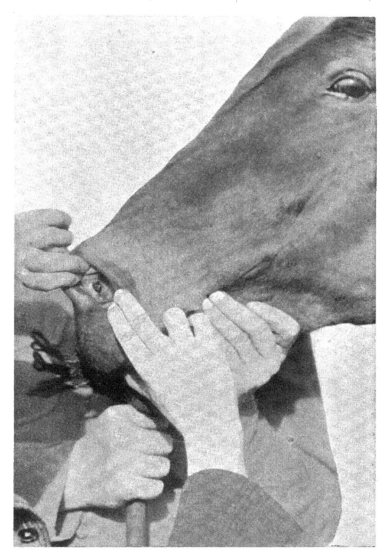

Shows the disease in an Indian country-bred horse.   On the nasal mucous membrane of
the left side, a single typical ulcer.   From a photograph taken in India.
Diagnosis verified by microscopical examination and
mallein testing.

PLATE XIV

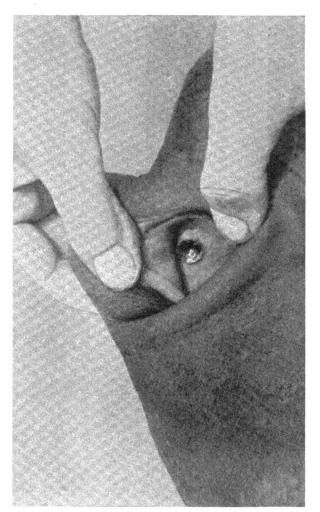

Shows a typical ulcer in an Arab stallion, on the nasal mucous membrane of the right side. This was first noticed exactly ten days previously as a small pimple which rapidly formed into a vesicle, broke on the third day and almost immediately assumed the appearance presented at the time the lesion was photographed. Diagnosis verified by microscopical examination.

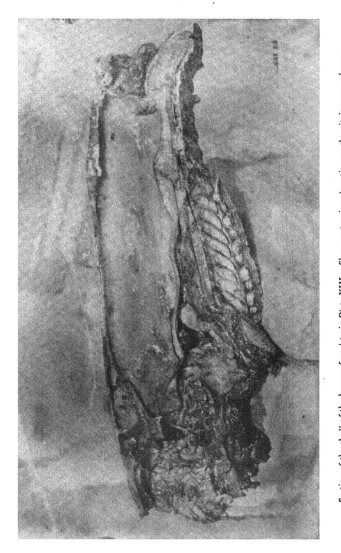

Section of the skull of the horse referred to in **Plate XIV**. Shows extensive ulceration on the pituitary membrane on the right side. From a photograph taken at the same time as the last, on which day the animal was destroyed.

PLATE XVI

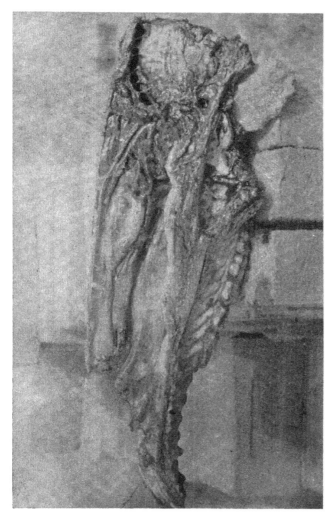

From the same case as Plates XIV and XV. Section of the skull showing extensive ulceration on the nasal mucous membrane of the left side, extending from underneath alae of nostril to membrane covering superior nasal chambers, turbinated bones, and sinuses of the head.

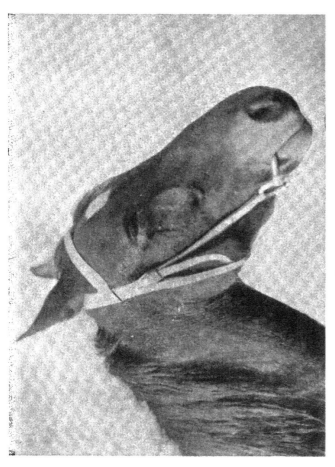

Shows the disease in an Indian country-bred horse. Extending from the conjunctiva of the right eye (the original seat of infection) along underneath the eye, backwards and upwards to the orbital process towards the base of the right ear. This case had the lesion on the inside of the eyelid for nearly two months before any external symptoms were apparent. From a photograph taken in India.

APPENDIX I

APPENDIX I

Circular to Local Authorities in Great Britain under the Diseases of Animals Acts, 1894 to 1903

BOARD OF AGRICULTURE AND FISHERIES
4 WHITEHALL PLACE
LONDON, S.W.
26th January, 1904

EPIZOOTIC LYMPHANGITIS OF THE HORSE

SIR

I am directed by the Board of Agriculture and Fisheries to acquaint you that it has been reported to them that a contagious disease of horses, known as ' epizootic lymphangitis,' has recently been detected in England and also in Ireland.

The symptoms of the disease are swelling of one of the limbs, usually a hind one, and the formation on the swollen member of small nodules which burst and discharge matter. In this respect the disease closely resembles ordinary farcy, from which, however, it may readily be distinguished by microscopic examination of the matter discharged from the sores, or by testing the horse with mallein.

The disease being of a very contagious character, it is important that cases, if any exist, should be detected at an early stage, and the Board therefore think it desirable to call the attention of Local Authorities to the danger which exists in this connexion.

The Board consider that the widest publicity should be given to the fact that every horse with a chronic ' thick leg ' on which sores are present is to be suspected of being affected either with epizootic lymphangitis or with farcy. Horse owners would be well advised to keep a special outlook for the development of such symptoms in the case of horses recently acquired by them. The Board would be glad to receive early information as to the existence or suspected existence of the disease in your district, should such information be available.

The Board will be happy to supply further copies of the present circular on hearing from you what number you require.

I am, Sir

Your obedient Servant

T. H. ELLIOTT

Secretary

THE CLERK TO THE
LOCAL AUTHORITY

ORDER OF THE BOARD OF AGRICULTURE AND FISHERIES

(DATED 5TH APRIL, 1904)

EPIZOOTIC LYMPHANGITIS ORDER OF 1904

The Board of Agriculture and Fisheries, by virtue and in exercise of the powers in them vested under the Diseases of Animals Acts, 1894 to 1903, and of every other power enabling them in this behalf, do order, and it is hereby ordered as follows :—

Separation of Diseased and Suspected Animals ;
Notice of Disease

1. (1) Every person having or having had in his possession or under his charge a horse affected with, or suspected of, epizootic lymphangitis shall (*a*) as far as practicable keep that horse separate from horses not so affected or suspected ; and (*b*) with all practicable speed give notice of the fact of the horse being so affected or suspected to a constable of the police force for the police area wherein the horse so affected, or suspected, is or was.

(2) Every person licensed to slaughter horses who has in his possession a carcase of any horse affected with epizootic lymphangitis shall with all practicable speed give notice of that fact to a constable of the police force for the police area wherein the carcase is.

(3) The constable receiving such notice shall forthwith give information of the receipt by him of the notice to an Inspector of the Local Authority, who shall forthwith report the same to the Local Authority.

(4) Where the notice of disease relates to a carcase of a horse that has died or been slaughtered in the district of a Local Authority other than the Local Authority which received the notice, the latter shall forthwith inform the other Local Authority of the receipt of the notice.

Duty of Inspector to act immediately

2. An Inspector of a Local Authority on receiving in any manner whatsoever information of the supposed existence of epizootic lymphangitis, or having reasonable ground to suspect the existence of such disease, shall proceed with all practicable speed to the place where such disease, according to the information received by him, exists, or is suspected to exist, and shall there and elsewhere put in force and discharge the powers and duties conferred and imposed on him as Inspector by or under the Act of 1894 and this Order.

Veterinary Inquiry by Local Authority as to existence of Epizootic Lymphangitis

3. (1) A Local Authority on receiving information of the existence, or supposed existence, of epizootic lymphangitis shall forthwith cause inquiry to be instituted as to the correctness of such information with the assistance and advice of a Veterinary Inspector, or of a veterinary practitioner qualified according to the Act of 1894 to be a Veterinary Inspector.

(2) The owner and occupier of any premises on which there is a horse affected with, or suspected of, epizootic lymphangitis, or the carcase of any such horse, shall give all reasonable facilities for the inquiry by the Local Authority under this Article, and any person failing to give such facilities shall be deemed guilty of an offence against the Act of 1894.

Prohibition of Movement by Inspector of Local Authority

4. (1) A Local Authority, on being satisfied by an inquiry under the preceding Article of the existence of epizootic lymphangitis, shall forthwith take such steps as may be practicable to secure the isolation of any horse affected with, or suspected of, that disease, and for that purpose an Inspector of a Local Authority may serve a Notice in writing (in the Form A set forth in the Schedule to this Order or to the like effect) on the owner or person in charge of any horse requiring that such horse be detained on or in any field, yard, stable, shed, or other place specified in the Notice, and after the service of such Notice it shall not be lawful for any person, while such Notice is in force—

(a) to move such horse from or out of such place of detention; or

(b) to permit any other horse to come in contact with any horse to which the Notice applies; or

(c) to remove from or out of such place any carcase of a horse, or any dung, fodder, litter, or other thing that has been in contact with any horse to which the Notice applies, without the written permission of an Inspector of the Local Authority.

(2) An Inspector of the Local Authority, if satisfied that the movement of any horse to which a Notice applies to some other place of detention is expedient for purposes of isolation or other necessary purposes, may serve a further similar Notice on the owner or person in charge of the horse requiring that the horse be detained on or in such other place, and thereupon such horse may be moved, subject to the directions of the Inspector, by the nearest available route and without unnecessary delay, to such place of detention, and, when so moved, shall be there detained and isolated in accordance with such further Notice.

(3) A Notice under this Article shall remain in force until it is withdrawn by a further Notice in writing (in the Form B set forth in the Schedule to this Order or to the like effect) signed by an Inspector of the Local Authority.

(4) An Inspector shall with all practicable speed send copies of any Notice served by him under this Article to the Local Authority, and to the police officer in charge of the nearest police station of the District, and also to the Board.

Provision as to Cleansing and Disinfection

5. (1) Any place in which a horse affected with, or suspected of, epizootic lymphangitis has been kept, and all utensils, mangers, feeding-troughs, pens, hurdles, harness, or other things used for or about such horse, shall, as soon as practicable, be cleansed and disinfected by, and at the expense of, the owner or occupier of such place as follows :—

(a) The place shall be swept out, and all litter, dung, or other thing that has been in contact with, or used about, any such horse shall forthwith be well mixed with quicklime and be effectually removed therefrom ; then

(b) The floor of the place and all other parts thereof with which such horse has come in contact shall be thoroughly washed, or scrubbed, or scoured, with water ; then

(c) The same parts of the place shall be washed over with lime-wash or some disinfectant approved by the Local Authority.

(*d*) In the case of a field, yard, or other place which is not capable of being so cleansed and disinfected, it shall be sufficient if such field, yard, or place be cleansed and disinfected so far as may be practicable.

(*e*) Every utensil, manger, feeding-trough, pen, hurdle, harness, or other thing used for or about such horse, shall, as soon as practicable after being so used and before being used for any other horse, be cleansed and disinfected by being thoroughly washed, or scrubbed, or scoured with water, and, where practicable, washed over with lime-wash, or with some disinfectant approved by the local Authority.

(2) If any person fails to cleanse and disinfect any place, or any utensil, manger, feeding trough, pen hurdle, harness, or other thing, in accordance with this Article, it shall be lawful for the Local Authority, without prejudice to the recovery of any penalty for the contravention of this Article, to cause such place or such utensil, manger, feeding-trough, pen, hurdle, harness, or other thing to be cleansed and disinfected, and to recover the expenses of such cleansing and disinfection from such person in any court of competent jurisdiction.

Disposal of Carcases

6. (1) The carcase of every horse that was affected with epizootic lymphangitis at the time when it died or was slaughtered shall be disposed of by the Local Authority as follows :

(i) Either the Local Authority shall cause the carcase to be buried as soon as possible in its skin in some proper place, and to be covered with a sufficient quantity of quicklime or other disinfectant, and with not less than six feet of earth ;

(ii) Or the Local Authority may, if authorized by Licence of the Board, cause the carcase to be destroyed, under the inspection of the Local Authority, in the mode following : The carcase shall be disinfected, and shall then be taken, in charge of an officer of the Local Authority, to premises approved for the purpose by the Board, and shall be there destroyed by exposure to a high temperature, or by chemical agents.

(2) With a view to the execution of the foregoing provisions of this Article the Local Authority may make such Regulations as they think fit for prohibiting or regulating the removal of any carcase of a horse, or for securing the burial or destruction of the same : Provided that the power to make Regulations under this Article shall be exercised only by the Local Authority or their Executive Committee and shall not be deputed to any other Committee or Sub-Committee.

(3) Where under this Article a Local Authority cause a carcase to be buried, they shall first cause its skin to be so slashed as to be useless.

(4) A Local Authority may cause or allow a carcase to be taken into the District of another Local Authority to be buried or destroyed, with the previous consent of that Local Authority or with a Licence in that behalf of the Board, but not otherwise.

Digging up

7. It shall not be lawful for any person, except with the Licence of an Inspector of the Board, to dig up, or cause to be dug up, the carcase of any horse that has been buried.

Powers of the Board of Agriculture and Fisheries

8. Any powers by this Order conferred upon a Local Authority or an Inspector of a Local Authority may at any time be exercised by the Board or an Inspector of the Board respectively.

Local Authority to enforce Order

2. The provisions of this Order, except where it is otherwise provided, shall be executed and enforced by the Local Authority.

Weekly Returns of Epizootic Lymphangitis

10. When an Inspector of a Local Authority finds epizootic lymphangitis in his district he shall forthwith make a return thereof to the Local Authority and to the Board, on a form provided by the Board, with all particulars therein required, and shall continue to so make a return thereof on the Saturday of every week until the disease has ceased.

Exemption of Army Veterinary Department and Veterinary Colleges

11. Nothing in this Order applies to horses in stables of military barracks or camps, if the horses are under the care and supervision of the Army Veterinary Department, or to horses in stables of any Veterinary College affiliated to the Royal College of Veterinary Surgeons : Provided that nothing in this Article shall be deemed to apply to the carcase of any horse, nor to exempt a Local Authority from any obligation imposed on them in regard to the disposal of carcases.

Offences

12. (1) If a horse, or carcase of a horse or other thing is moved in contravention of this Order, or of any Regulation made under this Order, or of a Notice given under this Order, the owner of the horse, carcase, or thing, and the person for the time being in charge thereof, and the person causing, directing, or permitting the movement, and the consignee or other person receiving or keeping it knowing it to have been moved in contravention as aforesaid, and the occupier of the place from which the horse, carcase, or thing is moved, shall, each according to and in respect of his own acts and defaults, be deemed guilty of an offence against the Act of 1894.

(2) If anything is omitted to be done as regards cleansing or disinfection in contravention of this Order, the owner and the lessee and the occupier and the person in charge of any place or thing in or in respect of which the same is omitted, shall, each according to and in respect of his own acts and defaults, be deemed guilty of an offence against the Act of 1894.

Extension of certain Sections of Diseases of Animals Act, 1894

13. Horses shall be animals, and epizootic lymphangitis shall be a disease, for the purposes of the following sections of the Act of 1894 (namely) :
Section forty-three (powers of police) ;
Section forty-four (powers of inspectors) ;
and also for the purposes of all other sections of the said Act containing provisions relative to or consequent on the provisions of those sections and this Order, including such sections as relate to offences or procedure.

Interpretation

14. In this Order, unless the context otherwise requires.—
' The Board ' means the Board of Agriculture and Fisheries :
' The Act of 1894 ' means the Diseases of Animals Act, 1894 :
' Inspector ' includes Veterinary Inspector :
' Carcase ' includes part of a carcase.
Other terms have the same meaning as in the Act of 1894.

Extent

15. This Order extends to England, Wales, and Scotland.

Commencement

16. This Order shall come into operation on the eighteenth day of April, nineteen hundred and four.

Short Title

17. This Order may be cited as the EPIZOOTIC LYMPHANGITIS ORDER OF 1904.

In witness whereof the Board of Agriculture and Fisheries have hereunto set their Official Seal this fifth day of April, nineteen hundred and four.

T. H. ELLIOTT, *Secretary*

———

SCHEDULE

FORM A

(Article 4)

Notice to Owner or Person in Charge of Horse Prohibiting Movement

DISEASES OF ANIMALS ACTS, 1894 TO 1903

EPIZOOTIC LYMPHANGITIS

To *A.B.* of

I, *C.D.*   , of   , being an Inspector appointed by the Local Authority of the [county] of   , hereby require the following horse, namely :
to be detained on or in [*here describe the field, yard, stable, shed, or other place where the horse is to be detained*] and I hereby require you to take notice that, in consequence of this Notice and the provisions of the Order of the Board of Agriculture and Fisheries under which this Notice is issued, it is not lawful for any person, until this Notice is withdrawn—

   (*a*) to move from or out of such place as aforesaid the horse to which this Notice applies ; or

   (*b*) to permit any other horse to come in contact with the horse to which this Notice applies ; or

   (*c*) to remove from or out of such place any carcase of a horse, or any dung, fodder, litter, or other thing that has been in contact with the horse to which this Notice applies, without the written permission of an Inspector of the Local Authority.

Dated this   day of   , 190 .

(*Signed*) C.D.

The Inspector is with all practicable speed to send copies of this Notice to the Local Authority and to the police officer in charge of the nearest police station of the district, and also to the Board of Agriculture and Fisheries, 4 Whitehall Place, London, S.W.

[*Read the Indorsement on this Notice*]

To be printed as Indorsement on Form A

The Order of the Board of Agriculture and Fisheries under which this Notice is issued provides that if a horse or carcase or thing is moved in contravention of such Order, or of this Notice, the owner of the horse, carcase, or thing, and the person for the time being in charge thereof, and the person causing, directing, or permitting the movement, and the consignee or other person receiving or keeping it knowing it to have been moved in contravention as aforesaid, and the occupier of the place from which the horse, carcase, or thing is moved, are liable under the Diseases of Animals Act, 1894, to the penalties thereby described.

Form B

(Article 4)

Withdrawal of Notice (Form A) to Owner or Person in charge of Horse Prohibiting Movement

DISEASES OF ANIMALS ACTS, 1894 to 1903

Epizootic Lymphangitis

To *A.B.* of

I, *C.D.*   of   , being an Inspector appointed by the Local Authority for the [county] of   , hereby withdraw, as from this   day of   , 190 , the Notice prohibiting movement signed by   and served upon you on the   day of   , of 190 .

Dated this   day of   , of 190 .

(*Signed*) C.D.

The Inspector is with all practicable speed to send copies of this Notice to the Local Authority and the police officer in charge of the nearest police station of the District, and also to the Board of Agriculture and Fisheries, 4 Whitehall Place, London, S.W.

APPENDIX II

DEPARTMENT OF AGRICULTURE AND
TECHNICAL INSTRUCTION FOR IRELAND
(VETERINARY BRANCH)

EPIZOOTIC LYMPHANGITIS

1. There has recently been introduced into Ireland a contagious disease known as epizootic lymphangitis, which affects horses, asses, and mules. It has for many years existed among horses in Italy, and in several other countries in Europe ; it is also prevalent in India and in some parts of South Africa.

2. The characteristic symptom of the disease consists of a swollen condition of the lymphatics of the skin on the inside of the hind legs, but the same condition may also be present on the side of the neck, or on the body. In most cases small nodules, varying in size from a pea to a hazel nut, will be found, which eventually burst and discharge a small quantity of purulent material containing an organism—the cryptoccus—which is the cause of the disease.

3. The cryptococcus when microsocopically examined presents itself as an ovid body, with a distinct double-contoured envelope and highly refractile contents. Owing to its considerable size and its characteristic form it is readily detected under a magnification of 400, and to this end it is not necessary to use any stain. The organism is easily transferred from the wound of a diseased horse to a wound on another horse not affected with this disease, and the most common means of such transfer is no doubt by the agency of sponges, rubbers, brushes, or other stable utensils, which have been used about diseased horses, or possibly by the hands of the attendant.

4. From the clinical symptoms epizootic lymphangitis may easily be mistaken for the farcy form of glanders : it can, however, be differentiated from that disease by a microscopical examination of some of the discharge from one of the ulcers, when the cryptococcus, which is the cause of the disease, will be found ; or by an application of the mallein test, to which epizootic lymphangitis does not respond.

5. In all instances where a case of epizootic lymphangitis is discovered the animal should at once be isolated, and separate implements should be used exclusively for the diseased animal.

6. Inasmuch as epizootic lymphangitis does not ordinarily lend itself to any known curative form of treatment, the owner would be well advised to slaughter the affected animal at once in order to prevent the disease being communicated to other animals in his possession or charge.

7. As the germs of the disease have been known to linger about a stable for a very considerable period, a rigid system of cleansing and disinfection should be applied to the whole of the stable or other place in which an affected horse has been kept, and all rubbers, sponges, brushes, and stable utensils used about affected horses should be burnt.

MATT. HEDLEY

Chief Inspector

DEPARTMENT OF AGRICULTURE AND TECHNICAL INSTRUCTION FOR IRELAND, VETERINARY BRANCH, CASTLE STREET DUBLIN, 22nd March, 1904

(No. 48)

ORDER OF THE DEPARTMENT OF AGRICULTURE AND TECHNICAL INSTRUCTION FOR IRELAND
(Dated 2nd May, 1904)

EPIZOOTIC LYMPHANGITIS (IRELAND) ORDER OF 1904

The Department of Agriculture and Technical Instruction for Ireland, by virtue and in exercise of the powers in them vested under the Agriculture and Technical Instruction (Ireland) Act, 1899, the Diseases of Animals Acts, 1894 to 1903, and of every other power enabling them in this behalf, do order, and it is hereby ordered as follows :—

Separation of Diseased and Suspected Animals ; Notice of Disease

1. (1) Every person having or having had in his possession or under his charge a horse, ass, or mule affected with, or suspected of, epizootic lymphangitis shall (*a*) as far as practicable keep that horse, ass, or mule separate from horses, asses, or mules not so affected or suspected ; and (*b*) with all practicable speed give notice of the fact of the horse, ass, or mule being so affected or suspected to a constable of the police force for the police area wherein the horse, ass, or mule so affected, or suspected, is or was.

(2) Every person licensed to slaughter horses, asses, or mules who has in his possession a carcase of any horse, ass, or mule affected with epizootic lymphangitis shall with all practicable speed give notice of that fact to a constable of the police force for the police area wherein the carcase is.

(3) The constable shall forthwith give information of the receipt by him of the notice to
   (i) The Secretary, Department of Agriculture and Technical Instruction for Ireland, Dublin ;
   (ii) An Inspector of the Local Authority ;
   (iii) The Local Authority.

H

(4) Where the notice of disease relates to a carcase of a horse, ass, or mule, that has died or been slaughtered in the district of a Local Authority other than the Local Authority which received the notice, the latter shall forthwith inform the other Local Authority of the receipt of the notice.

Duty of Inspector to act immediately

2. An Inspector of a Local Authority on receiving in any manner whatsoever information of the supposed existence of epizootic lymphangitis, or having reasonable ground to suspect the existence of such disease, shall proceed with all practicable speed to the place where such disease, according to the information received by him, exists, or is suspected to exist, and shall there and elsewhere put in force and discharge the powers and duties conferred and imposed on him as Inspector by or under the Act of 1894 and this Order.

Veterinary Inquiry by Local Authority as to existence of Epizootic Lymphangitis

3. (1) A Local Authority on receiving information of the existence, or supposed existence, of epizootic lymphangitis shall forthwith cause inquiry to be instituted as to the correctness of such information with the assistance and advice of a Veterinary Inspector, or of veterinary practitioner qualified according to the Act of 1894 to be a Veterinary Inspector.

(2) The owner or occupier of any premises on which there is a horse, ass, or mule affected with, or suspected of epizootic lymphangitis, or the carcase of any such horse, ass, or mule, shall give all reasonable facilities for the inquiry by the Local Authority under this Article, and any person failing to give such facilities shall be deemed guilty of an offence against the Act of 1894.

Prohibition of Movement by Inspector of Local Authority

4. (1) A Local Authority, on being satisfied by an inquiry under the preceding Article of the existence of epizootic lymphangitis shall forthwith take such steps as may be practicable to secure the isolation of any horse, ass, or mule affected with, or suspected of, that disease, and for that purpose an Inspector of a Local Authority may serve a Notice in writing (in the Form A set forth in the Schedule to this Order or to the like effect) on the owner or person

in charge of any horse, ass, or mule requiring that such horse, ass, or mule, be detained on or in any field, yard, stable, shed, or other place specified in the Notice, and after the service of such Notice it shall not be lawful for any person, while such Notice is in force—

(a) To move such horse, ass, or mule from or out of such place of detention ; or

(b) To permit any other horse, ass, or mule to come in contact with any horse, ass, or mule to which the Notice applies ; or

(c) To remove from out of such place any carcase of a horse, ass, or mule, or any dung, fodder, litter, or other thing that has been in contact with any horse, ass, or mule, to which the Notice applies, without the written permission of an Inspector of the Local Authority.

(2) An Inspector of the Local Authority, if satisfied that the movement of any horse, ass, or mule to which a Notice applies to some other place of detention is expedient for purposes of isolation or other necessary purpose, may serve a further similar Notice on the owner or person in charge of the horse, ass, or mule requiring that the horse, ass, or mule be detained on or in such other place, and thereupon such horse, ass, or mule may be moved, subject to the directions of the Inspector, by the nearest available route and without unnecessary delay, to such place of detention, and, when so moved, shall be there detained and isolated in accordance with such further notice.

3. A Notice under this Article shall remain in force until it is withdrawn by a further Notice in writing (in the Form B set forth in the Schedule to this Order or to the like effect) signed by an Inspector of the Local Authority.

(4) An Inspector shall with all practicable speed send copies of any Notice served by him under this Article to—

(i) The Secretary, Department of Agriculture and Technical Instruction for Ireland, Dublin ;

(ii) The Local Authority ;

(iii) The Police Officer in charge of the nearest police station of the District.

Provision as to Cleansing and Disinfection

5. (1) Any place in which a horse, ass, or mule affected with, or suspected of, epizootic lymphangitis has been kept, and all utensils, mangers, feeding-troughs, pens, hurdles, harness, or other things

used for or about such horse, ass, or mule shall, as soon as practicable, be cleansed and disinfected by, and at the expense of, the owner or occupier of such place as follows :—

(*a*) The place shall be swept out, and all litter, dung, or other thing that has been in contact with, or used about, any such horse, ass, or mule, shall forthwith be well mixed with quicklime and be effectually removed therefrom ; then

(*b*) The floor of the place and all other parts thereof with which such horse, ass, or mule has come in contact shall be thoroughly washed, or scrubbed, or scoured with water ; then

(*c*) The same parts of the place shall be washed over with lime-wash or some disinfectant approved by the Local Authority.

(*d*) In the case of a field, yard, or other place which is not capable of being so cleansed and disinfected, it shall be sufficient if such field, yard, or place be cleansed and disinfected so far as may be practicable.

(*e*) Every utensil, manger, feeding-trough, pen, hurdle, harness, or other thing used for or about such horse, ass, or mule, shall, as soon as practicable after being so used and before being used for any other horse, ass, or mule, be cleansed and disinfected by being thoroughly washed, or scrubbed, or scoured, with water, and, where practicable, washed over with lime-wash, or with some disinfectant approved by the Local Authority.

(2) If any person fails to cleanse and disinfect any place, or any utensil, manger, feeding-trough, pen, hurdle, harness, or other thing, in accordance with this Article, it shall be lawful for the Local Authority, without prejudice to the recovery of any penalty for the contravention of this article, to cause such place or such utensil, manger, feeding-trough, pen, hurdle, harness, or other thing to be cleansed and disinfected, and to recover the expenses of such cleansing and disinfection from such person in any court of competent jurisdiction.

Movement of Horses, Asses, or Mules, etc., with Special Licence

6. Notwithstanding anything in this Order, any horse, ass, or mule, carcase, or thing may be moved in any circumstance with a Licence of an inspector of, or other officer authorized by, the Department, which Licence will only be granted where the Department, after inquiry, are satisfied that exceptional circumstances render the movement necessary or expedient.

Disposal of Carcases

7. (1) The carcase of every horse, ass, or mule that was affected with epizootic lympangitis at the time when it died or was slaughtered shall be disposed of by the Local Authority as follows :—

(i) Either the Local Authority shall cause the carcase to be buried as soon as possible in its skin in some proper place, and to be covered with a sufficient quantity of quicklime or other disinfectant, and with not less than six feet of earth ;

(ii) Or the Local Authority may, if authorized by Licence of the Department, cause the carcase to be destroyed, under the inspection of the Local Authority, in the mode following :— The carcase shall be disinfected, and shall then be taken, in charge of an officer of the Local Authority to premises approved for the purpose by the Department, and shall be there destroyed by exposure to a high temperature, or by chemical agents.

(2) With a view to the execution of the foregoing provisions of this Article the Local Authority may make such regulations as they think fit for prohibiting or regulating the removal of any carcase of a horse, ass, or mule, or for securing the burial or destruction of the same : Provided that the power to make Regulations under this Article shall be exercised only by the Local Authority or their Executive Committee, and shall not be deputed to any other Committee or Sub-Committee.

(3) Where under this Article a Local Authority cause a carcase to be buried, they shall first cause its skin to be so slashed as to be useless.

(4) A Local Authority may cause or allow a carcase to be taken into the district of another Local Authority to be buried or destroyed, with the previous consent of that Local Authority or with a Licence in that behalf of the Department, but not otherwise.

Digging up

8. It shall not be lawful for any person, except with the Licence of an Inspector of the Department, to dig up, or cause to be dug up, the carcase of any horse that has been buried.

Powers of the Department

9. Any powers by this Order conferred upon a Local Authority or an Inspector of Local Authority may at any time be exercised by the Department or an Inspector of the Department respectively.

Local Authority to enforce Order

10. The provisions of this Order, except where it is otherwise provided, shall be executed and enforced by the Local Authority.

Weekly Returns of Epizootic Lymphangitis

11. When an Inspector of a Local Authority finds epizootic lymphangitis in his district, he shall forthwith make a return thereof to the Local Authority and to the Department, on a form provided by the Department, with all particulars therein required, and shall continue to so make a return thereof on the Saturday of every week until the disease has ceased.

Exemption of Army Veterinary Department and Veterinary Colleges

12. Nothing in this Order applies to horses, asses, or mules in stables of military barracks or camps, if the horses, asses, or mules are under the care and supervision of the Army Veterinary Department, or to horses, asses, or mules in stables of any Veterinary College affiliated to the Royal College of Veterinary Surgeons : Provided that nothing in this Article shall be deemed to apply to the carcase of any horse, ass, or mule, nor to exempt a Local Authority from any obligation imposed on them in regard to the disposal of carcases.

Offences

13. (1) If a horse, ass, or mule, or carcase of a horse, ass, or mule, or other thing is moved in contravention of this Order, or of any Regulation made under this Order, or of a Notice given under this Order, the owner of the horse, ass, or mule, carcase, or thing, and the person for the time being in charge thereof, and the person causing, directing, or permitting the movement, and the consignee or other person receiving or keeping it knowing it to have been moved in contravention as aforesaid, and the occupier of the place from which the horse, ass, or mule, carcase, or thing is moved, shall each according to and in respect of his own acts and defaults, be deemed guilty of an offence against the Act of 1894.

(2) If anything is omitted to be done as regards cleansing or disinfection in contravention of this Order, the owner and the lessee and the occupier and the person in charge of any place or thing in or in respect of which the same is omitted, shall, each according to and in respect of his own acts and defaults, be deemed guilty of an offence against the Act of 1894.

Extension of certain Sections of Diseases of Animals Acts, 1894

14. Horses, asses, or mules shall be animals, and epizootic lymphangitis shall be a disease, for the purposes of the following sections of the Act of 1894 (namely) :—

> Section forty-three (powers of police) ;
> Section forty-four (powers of inspectors) ;

and also for the purposes of all other sections of the said Act containing provisions relative to or consequent on the provisions of those sections and this Order, including such sections as relate to offences or procedure.

Interpretation

15. In this Order, unless the context otherwise requires—

'The Act of 1894' means the Diseases of Animal Act, 1894 :

'The Department' means the Department of Agriculture and Technical Instruction for Ireland :

'Inspector' includes Veterinary Inspector :

'Carcase' includes part of a carcase :

Other terms have the same meaning as in the Act of 1894.

Extent

16. This Order extends to the whole of Ireland.

Commencement

17. This Order shall come into operation on the twentieth day of May, one thousand nine hundred and four.

Short Title

18. This Order may be cited as the EPIZOOTIC LYMPHANGITIS (IRELAND) ORDER OF 1904.

In witness whereof the Department of Agriculture and Technical Instruction for Ireland have hereunto set their official Seal this Second day of May, one thousand nine hundred and four.

T. P. GILL

Secretary

SCHEDULE

Form A

(Article 4)

Notice to Owner or Person in Charge of Horse, Ass, or Mule, Prohibiting Movement

DISEASES OF ANIMALS ACTS, 1894 TO 1903

Epizootic Lymphangitis

To *A.B.* of

I, *C.D.*   , of   , being an Inspector appointed by the Local Authority of the [county] of , [or being an Inspector of the Department of Agriculture and Technical Instruction for Ireland], hereby require the following horse, ass, or mule, namely :

to be detained on or in [*here describe the field, yard, stable, shed, or other place where the horse, ass, or mule is to be detained*] and I hereby require you to take notice that, in consequence of this Notice and the provisions of the Order under which this Notice is issued, it is not lawful for any person, until this Notice is withdrawn—

(*a*) to move from or out of such place as aforesaid any horse, ass, or mule to which this Notice applies ;

(*b*) to permit any other horse, ass, or mule to come in contact with the horse, ass, or mule to which this Notice applies ; or

(*c*) to remove from or out of such place any carcase of a horse, ass, or mule, or any dung, fodder, litter, or other thing that has been in contact with the horse, ass, or mule, to which this Notice applies, without the written permission of an Inspector of the Local Authority.

Dated this   day of   , 190 .

(Signed) C.D.

The Inspector giving this Notice is with all practicable speed to send copies of this Notice to

(i) The Secretary, Department of Agriculture and Technical Instruction for Ireland, Dublin ;

(ii) The Local Authority ;

(iii) The Police Officer in charge of the nearest police station of the District.

[*Read the Indorsement on this Notice*]

To be printed as Indorsement on Form A

The Order under which this Notice is issued provides that if a horse, ass, or mule, or carcase, or thing is moved in contravention of such Order, or of this Notice, the owner of the horse, ass, or mule, carcase, or thing, and the person for the time being in charge thereof, and the person causing, directing, or permitting the movement, and the consignee or other person receiving or keeping it knowing it to have been moved in contravention as aforesaid, and the occupier of the place from which the horse, ass, or mule, carcase, or thing is moved, are liable under the Diseases of Animals Act, 1894, to the penalties thereby prescribed.

Form B

(Article 4)

Withdrawal of Notice (Form A) to Owner or Person in charge of Horse, Ass, or Mule, Prohibiting Movement

DISEASES OF ANIMALS ACTS, 1894 to 1903

Epizootic Lymphangitis

To *A.B.* of

I, *C.D.* , of , being
an Inspector appointed by the Local Authority of the (county) of
[or being an
Inspector of the Department of Agriculture and Technical Instruction
for Ireland], hereby withdraw as from this day of
19 , the Notice prohibiting movement, signed by
and served upon you on the day of 19 .
Dated this day of , 19 .

(*Signed*) C.D.

Copies of this Notice are to be sent with all practicable speed to
  (i) The Secretary, Department of Agriculture and Technical Instruction for Ireland, Dublin ;
  (ii) The Local Authority ;
  (iii) The Police Officer in charge of the nearest police station of the district.

INDEX

INDEX

www.ingramcontent.com/pod-product-compliance
Lightning Source LLC
Chambersburg PA
CBHW071214050326
40689CB00011B/2328